Praise Now! 2

More Ready-to-Use Services for Contemporary and Multisensory Worship

Nylea L. Butler-Moore
Nancy C. Townley

Abingdon Press
Nashville

PRAISE NOW! 2
MORE READY-TO-USE SERVICES FOR CONTEMPORARY AND MULTISENSORY WORSHIP

Copyright © 2004 by Abingdon Press

This book is printed on acid-free, recycled paper.

ISBN 0-687-07478-9

04 05 06 07 08 09 10 11 12 13 — 10 9 8 7 6 5 4 3 2 1

MANUFACTURED IN THE UNITED STATES OF AMERICA

Contents

With Grateful Hearts

The authors wish to thank the following people for their support and help:
- Our husbands, Jim Townley and Kyle Butler-Moore, and Nylea's daughter Haley for their patience, love, and support during this process of creation.
- Jim Townley for helping with the Internet transmission of E-mail and file attachments from New York to California.
- Lesley Leonard and Jerry and Barbara Popp, who worked tirelessly on the visual designs, lugging heavy items, creating wonderful things for worship, loaning us the many supplies and items to complete worship settings, and then cleaning up the sanctuary at St. Paul's UMC when the photograph session concluded.
- Bud's Florist and Greenhouse in Castleton, New York. The proprietor, Judy, was very generous in lending us many lush plants for our visual designs, as well as some of the seasonal artificial plants we needed.
- Alan and Suzanne Metzger, Karen Townley Carr, Kirk and Jean Duncan and little Hannah, Lesley Leonard, and many others who let us tell their stories of faith and celebration.
- God, who has given us all these wonderful people, who has opened vistas of creativity, who has supported us and encouraged us during this endeavor and throughout our lives.

All praise and glory be to God and to our Lord Jesus Christ! Amen.

What's It All About?

Have you ever thought about doing something different in your worship services? Maybe you've heard or read about worship renewal and various worship styles. Perhaps you wonder if a change is needed in your congregation's worship, and if so, how to begin making that change. We hope this resource will help as a "starting place" for planning multisensory worship (worship that uses many senses) or as a springboard for developing your own ideas and implementing the unique skills, gifts, and talents of your congregation.

Ready-to-Use Services

Praise Now! 2 features twenty ready-to-use, multisensory worship services. The services are suitable for churches of all sizes, especially the small- to medium-sized church that has never tried multisensory worship but is considering it.

Each service has been designed with the prayerful hope that those in attendance, from the nonbeliever to the seasoned worshiper, will experience God's Word and presence. The theme is chosen for its relevance to today's world and its ability to resonate with people of many ages and cultural backgrounds.

Each worship service follows the same basic format:

• Theme, scripture reference(s), title, and time in the Christian Year when the service is most appropriate
• An outline of the service, especially helpful for use in generating a worship bulletin or a worship order for leaders
• A complete "fleshed out" service, including prayers, drama skits, music and video clip suggestions, and points to aid in message/sermon development
• A list of resources used in the service and additional resources that may be used in lieu of or in conjunction with the primary resources
• Corresponding visual designs, as suggested in the "Visual Designs, Displays, and Resources" section on page 10 of this guide

The services last approximately one hour each. Depending upon a variety of factors, such as resources used, tempos of musical selections, speed of delivery of the spoken word, the amount of time needed to collect the offering and for sitting, standing, and moving through the worship space, the services may run shorter or longer than sixty minutes. Encourage congregants to become "Spirit watchers" rather than "clock watchers" and to put aside the things that distract them from entering into worship.

No single worship model or worship service suits all churches. Although the services presented in *Praise Now! 2* are ready to use, you may find the need to adapt the services to fit your congregation's situation.

Components of Worship

While the flow of worship may vary from service to service, most of the elements in each service are the same. These worship components include: Musical Invitation; Call to Worship; Worship Focus; Congregational Songs; Video Clips, Skits, and Interpretive Movement; Presentation Pieces; Message Movers; Prayer Time; Opportunities for Service; Offering; Sending Forth; and Visuals (suggestions for displays and designs).

1. Musical Invitation

The musical invitation is sometimes called "Gathering Music" in a contemporary or blended service, or "Prelude" in a traditional service. This musical selection, which can be either instrumental or vocal, helps to set the mood for the service and begins drawing people into worship. Ideally, it should be thought of as the first element in the worship service, rather than something that precedes worship. The individuals who regularly lead the worship music usually offer the musical invitation, but other musicians and musical groups in the church may provide it on occasion. Another option is to play one or more selections from a CD recording.

2. Call to Worship

Typically a responsorial reading for Leader (L) and People (P), the call to worship does just that—it calls people to worship. It also helps set up the theme for the service.

3. Worship Focus

The worship focus is a brief statement or responsorial reading that conveys the theme for the day. It helps the worshiper to understand the direction the service will be taking.

4. Congregational Songs

Congregational singing has always played an important role in worship. Not only does congregational singing engage the congregation physically, mentally, and emotionally, it also transmits theology and unites a worshiping body, giving it a "voice."

5. Video Clips, Skits, and Interpretive Movement

Drama, both spoken and unspoken, is a powerful means of conveying God's Word. Not only are video clips, skits, and interpretive movement entertaining, they can effectively drive home the message/theme of the service. They also speak to a culture that is, according to statistics, overwhelmingly visually stimulated.

When a video clip is suggested, you will notice a listing of the format used and "start" and "stop" times to aid you in locating the clip. These numbers may or may not coincide exactly with the counter on your equipment, but should enable you to locate the clip fairly easily. All of the videos are available in both VHS and DVD formats, so the start and stop times will vary depending on the format used.

6. Presentation Pieces

Presentation pieces are musical selections that are usually not suitable for congregational singing, although a presentation piece may be used as a vehicle for introducing a new song to a congregation. Worship music leaders, choirs, special musical guests, and so forth offer these pieces. In more traditional services, presentation pieces are called often "introits" and "anthems."

7. Message Movers

In this resource, the assumption is made that the pastor typically delivers the message or sermon. However, any competent speaker in your congregation may provide the message. Message movers are basic points upon which the speaker may build/develop the message in keeping with the theme of the service.

8. Prayer Time

Spending time in prayer is an essential component of corporate worship. During prayer time, we offer praise for who God is, for God's reconciling acts of goodness and mercy, and for the many blessings in our lives. We ask for forgiveness, and we pray for ourselves, for one another, for the community, and for the world.

If no specific prayers are listed for a particular service, develop prayer time as desired. If one prayer is listed, use it at the end of prayer time, or when it seems to work best.

9. Opportunities for Service

The opportunities for service are most frequently called the "announcements" and are often thought of as business to get out of the way. The worship designers of this resource have elevated the announcements to opportunities for congregants to act out their faith through the ministries of the church. Service and ministry are the key words here.

10. Offering

Like the opportunities for service, the offering is often thought of as "taking care of the business of the church"—in this case, the financial business. But collecting the offering is much more than a weekly financial obligation. Giving out of our abundance (or even out of a lack of abundance) is a response to God's numerous gifts to us. Like the opportunities for service, the offering provides a chance for us to support the ministries of the church and to share God's love with others through our monetary giving.

11. Sending Forth

In a more traditional worship setting, the sending forth is often called the "blessing and benediction." Typically, the pastor or the worship leader offers the sending forth at the end of the worship service.

12. Visuals

As the worshiper enters the worship space prior to the beginning of the service, he or she will likely notice a visual display or design that enhances the theme and message of the service. Visuals may be focused on the central table or encompass the whole worship area. See the photographs (1-20) in the insert of this book. Each photograph corresponds to the worship service with the same number.

Forming a Worship Team

Because the multisensory worship experience involves a number of diverse elements and technologies, it cannot be successfully planned and executed by only one or two persons. A worship team is necessary. This team should meet on a regular basis to brainstorm and share ideas, create worship services, and evaluate services after they have been experienced.

Who should be part of the worship team? Before you answer this question, carefully consider the scope of the worship services you want to implement and the main components you want to incorporate into those services. Sometimes less is definitely better! For example, you don't have to have full-blown multimedia, a worship band, an actors' guild, and theater lighting and sound. Take into account the skills and talents of congregants, their time availability, and your worship budget. Then select at least one person to represent each of the worship elements you have chosen. These people may form their own subcommittees. See elements listed above.

You may also wish to include one or two congregants who have a passion for worship. Emphasize that they do not have to be skilled in worship planning; this is something they will learn as they participate in the team. Their perspectives as members of the worshiping congregation can be an invaluable resource.

The core of the worship team should consist of those persons who actually lead the congregation in worship each week. A full-fledged multisensory worship team could consist of: pastor, worship leader, music director, drama leader, interpretive movement coordinator, visuals leader, and members of the technology crew.

Leaders and Their Roles

Each church situation is different, and no two people have the same set of skills and experience. Consequently, you may find that developing a full-fledged worship team isn't possible for your congregation. Just because you don't have all these people on your team doesn't mean you can't do multisensory worship. It simply means that your multisensory worship experience should use the gifts and talents you *do* have. Use the brief descriptions listed below to help you develop your worship team. Note that the descriptions are only "beginning points" for the persons who fill those roles, and that the roles will develop over time.

PASTOR

The pastor is charged with the responsibility for the worship life of the congregation, either by creating the services and taking a major role in them, or by working with a worship team to create meaningful worship services for the congregation. The pastor's work with the team is essential. Through the pastor's theological training, he or she can offer insight into specific scriptures and doctrine, which will be critical to work of the worship music leaders and the worship art planners. Generally, the pastor is considered to be the person who delivers the message, and conducts the sacraments of the church (Baptism and Holy Communion). However, in many denominations, including The United Methodist Church, certified lay speakers can fill the role of pastor with the exception of sacramental work.

WORSHIP LEADER

The worship leader facilitates the flow of worship and acts as an "interface" between the service and the congregants. He or she is a model of transparent worship who makes segues between various components of the service; leads prayers; shows the congregation when to stand, sit, and move. In other words, this person is one who, by his or her own worship of God, helps the service flow smoothly. The worship leader could be the pastor, the primary musician, or both. Sometimes the leader is a third person. In any event, the leader(s) should be uniquely gifted to fulfill this important role. These gifts include: an ease at being in front of others and in leading worship, a pleasant stage presence, an ability to "think on your feet," and a discerning spirit that can sense the Spirit's moving in a service and adapt as necessary.

MUSIC DIRECTOR

The music director is the person who is ultimately in charge of the music within the service. This person may be the director of music ministries, the band leader, the choir director, the keyboard player, or the lead vocalist. Selecting, preparing, rehearsing, and presenting music are major responsibilities of the music director. When the congregational worship music is chosen, the music director also assists in the weekly preparation of slides or transparencies of lyrics. In many cases, the church secretary or a person skilled in the use of technology will be the one who completes the task. See "Technology Crew" below.

DRAMA LEADER

The drama leader should be a resource person who suggests dramas for worship, and finds the actors and rehearses with them. This person should have theatrical and staging experience and be able to envision dramatic possibilities within the worship space.

INTERPRETIVE MOVEMENT COORDINATOR

Movement can encompass a wide range of physical motion, such as standing, sitting, coming forward to receive communion, simple hand/body motions to a particular song, and elements of interpretive dance. This worship team member should have dance experience and be able to envision simple ways to engage the congregation through movement. This person should also be able to develop interpretive dances that would be presented with one, two, or several dancers.

VISUALS LEADER

All visuals (including banners, communion table settings, and so on) should relate directly to the theme of the particular worship service for which they are designed. Choose a person for this position who understands the basic elements of artistic design and who has a flare for creating visual displays. This may be the head of your altar guild or someone else in your congregation. The visual arts team should work closely with the pastor or the person (or persons) who design specific worship services in order to give a uniform visual presentation.

TECHNOLOGY CREW

Some small- to medium-sized churches would be alarmed at the mention of a technology crew. They would expect that people with expertise in high-tech areas would be needed, and their congregations may not have such persons available. It is important to note that *Praise Now! 2* is very flexible. Much of the worship material can be accomplished with the use of simple equipment. Do not let the concept of a technology crew prohibit you from using this resource.

Determine whether your church is low tech or high tech regarding projecting texts and graphics, showing video clips, playing CDs, and running a sound system. Examine the equipment you have and the people skilled in using the equipment. Do you use an overhead projector with transparencies; a slide projector; or a laptop computer loaded with PowerPoint®, Media Shout, or other software, and an Internet link? Do you show video clips (VHS or DVD) and play CDs? Do you use a simple or sophisticated sound system in worship, or have no sound system? If you need to purchase new or additional equipment, what is your budget?

The head of the technology crew should be someone who is skilled in the use of the aforementioned equipment and is able to train others. A small group of people working under the guidance of a tech leader is ideal. Depending upon the scope of your technology area, you may wish to subdivide the tech category into several teams (such as graphics, sound, video and CD) with a chairperson overseeing the complete work area.

Time Issues

In most churches, most of the people serving on the worship team will be unpaid volunteers who have full-time jobs outside of the church. Time availability may be a big factor regarding their participation in the committee. If this is true in your situation, consider meeting once a month with the entire committee and weekly with a smaller core group (perhaps comprised of the pastor, the music director, and the worship leader). The smaller group would take minutes of its meetings and distribute them to the members who cannot attend regular meetings. Regular communication between the small group and the large group is essential. Try setting up a group E-mail list, and designate one person as the "secretary," who will forward worship information to all members.

Licenses Needed

Photo copiers, CD burners, computers, and other duplicating devices have made it extremely easy to illegally reproduce copyrighted works of art, music, and film. Unfortunately, many churches are quite lax in their use of copyrighted materials, perhaps not realizing that these materials are someone's property. When that property is used without paying the owner, the property has been stolen. Certainly the church should not be engaged in acts of stealing! When artists are not financially compensated for their work, they are denied part of their livelihoods; their publishers face the possibility of not being able to publish materials due to lack of revenue.

So, if you plan to print or project song lyrics and hymn texts for your congregation, make arrangements of songs that have no published version, show video clips during worship, and/or record your worship services, you need to secure inexpensive licenses to allow you to do so legally. These licenses are available through CCLI (Christian Copyright Licensing International); CVLI (Christian Video Licensing International); and CVLI's sister company, MPLC (The Motion Picture Licensing Corporation).

CCLI—Use of Songs and Hymns

CCLI's mission is "to encourage the spirit of worship through music to the local church collectively and to Christians individually, so that they may enhance their corporate worship expression spontaneously, conveniently, affordably, and legally." In order to fulfill its mission, CCLI offers several licenses to the local church.

The most popular license is "The Church Copyright License," which features legal access to more than 150,000 songs for congregational use. After paying an annual fee based on your church's total average weekly worship attendance, you receive a license that grants you permission to access CCLI's "Authorized List." You may make, from this body of materials, overhead transparencies, song sheets and songbooks; input lyrics on a computer; record worship services; and make arrangements of music where no published version exists.

The license does not convey the right to duplicate music for worship teams—one legal copy of the music must be purchased for each team member. It does not allow you to reproduce choral music, keyboard arrangements, vocal solos, or instrumental works. Legal copies must be purchased. If a work is "out-of-print," permission to reproduce must be obtained from the copyright holder.

CCLI also offers a lead sheet service, which allows you to search for and download lead sheets (melody line and guitar chords) of authorized songs; and the SongSelect Lyric Service, which enables you to download lyrics directly into PowerPoint® or other computer program. To learn more about other CCLI services and licenses, contact CCLI at: Christian Copyright Licensing International, 17201 N.E. Sacramento, Portland, OR 97230, 1-800-234-2446, www.ccli.com.

CVLI and MPLC—Use of Motion Picture Videocassettes and Videodiscs

Commonly available in retail or rental stores, VHS and DVD copies of motion pictures are intended for home use only. As based on the Copyright Act of 1976, viewing videos outside the home requires a license—even for nonprofit organizations, even if no admission is charged, and even if the video has been legally purchased.

CCLI's website contains a link to CVLI, which is CCLI's counterpart for legal use of video recordings. "The Church Video License" provides legal coverage for churches to show home movies (VHS or DVD) for a variety of church activities, including worship services. MPLC, CVLI's sister company, offers the "Umbrella License," which allows unlimited use of all MPLC authorized motion picture titles within licensed facilities, such as your church.

CVLI, in conjunction with CCLI, also offers a service called "Screen Vue." For a yearly fee, you will receive five DVDs with over 200 one- to four-minute film clips suitable for sermon and teaching illustration. A CVLI license is needed to show these clips legally. Visit www.screenvue.com for more information. You can also visit www.us.imdb.com to access "The Internet Movie Database." Thousands of films are catalogued here, and the site has a powerful search tool that lets you key in plot summaries, character names, movies ratings, titles, key words or quotes, and much more. It is the closest thing to a "motion picture concordance" available.

To learn more about CVLI and MPLC services, contact:

Christian Video Licensing International
17201 N.E. Sacramento
Portland, OR 97230
1-888-771-2854 or *1-800-234-2446
www.cvl.org

The Motion Picture Licensing Corporation
5455 Centinela Avenue
Los Angeles, CA 90066-6970
1-800-462-8855
www.mplc.com

*(*You can contact CCLI to get both CCLI and CVLI licenses and information, as the offices for both organizations are located in the same building.)*

Resource Information Correct?

At the time of publication, resource information, including product availability, web addresses, product numbers, and so forth, was correct. Please note that over time, this information may change, especially Internet site listings. If you are unable to locate a resource, try using a web search engine or contacting your local Christian bookstore.

So, What's It All About?

So, what's this resource really all about? In a word, it is about worship—giving praise and honor to God. It is about encountering God and one another in our worship services; finding forgiveness, strength, renewal, acceptance; being active, rather than passive, participants; building community; being fed, nourished, and challenged; and taking our faith into the world.

While *Praise Now! 2* encourages the use of multi-sensory worship elements and various technologies, it is critical to remember that these things are vehicles to worship, not ends in themselves. These tools can enable us to experience God's presence in new and exciting ways. At the same time, worship can occur in the simplest of services. We must be true to our calling and God-given gifts when planning and leading worship. So, don't be afraid to start small, but think big—offer your gifts in service to God and expect great things to happen!

Visual Designs, Displays, and Resources

Nancy C. Townley

From earliest human history, humankind has communicated in pictures, symbolic representations of home, hunt, and community. These pictures—found in caves in France, in the sophisticated hieroglyphs of Egypt, in the cliff art of southwestern America, and in ancient oriental writings—were all ways in which people made their ideas, dreams, and hopes known to one another.

The medieval cathedrals in Europe housed incredible stained glass art that tell the stories of the faith. The altars, chancels, and chapels became repositories of exquisite paintings, sculpture, needlework, and other artistic representations of religious faith.

Perhaps the most familiar symbol for the Christian is the cross. Depicted in about eighty different forms, the cross forms an instantly recognizable symbol for Jesus, salvation, sacrifice, and resurrection. An instrument of degradation and torture, it has become the centrally adored symbol in Christianity.

We are surrounded by imagery in today's world. Advertisers have developed a multitude of symbols, and we have dutifully learned to identify their products by that symbol. Often a special song accompanies the graphic symbol, assisting the consumer in remembering and purchasing the product.

Our traffic patterns and driving are controlled by symbols: the octagonal stop sign, the triangular yield sign, the square yellow signs that provide information about road conditions and configurations. Street signs, symbols for our churches (such as the "cross and flame logo" for The United Methodist Church), the large "H" for hospitals, and the pedestrian traffic signs are part of our daily lives.

Many books have been written about religious symbolism, colors, and customs. It is not within the scope of *Praise Now! 2* to elaborate on these things. However, we hope the resource will spark the creativity of persons in local churches regarding the use of symbolism, colors, and customs in worship. Through art in the worship space, the spoken word, the prayed word, and the sung word are connected in a multisensory way.

Designs for Worship Services in *Praise Now! 2*

As with the worship service plans in *Praise Now! 2*, feel free to change the visual design plans to suit your congregation's needs. Make the settings your own. You do not have to spend a large amount of money to create the visual displays in this resource. Borrow as much as you can, and look for different uses for the same objects. For example, the basket used in the Palm/Passion Sunday display for Service 10 was used again in Service 19 for the communion bread.

It is not necessary to purchase individual fabrics or items for each worship service. A ten-yard piece of purple cotton fabric was used in at least eight services; and the white, green, and black fabrics, the landscaper's burlap, and the tightly woven burlap were used in a variety of settings. The same candles, rocks, wood, and banners were used in several displays. A large number of beautiful houseplants were on loan from Bud's Florist and Greenhouse.

Holy Hardware

What is "Holy Hardware"? Simply put, it is the tools and supplies of the liturgical visual artist. As you gather supplies for visual designs and displays, you begin to establish a "Holy Hardware" collection. You will use these items on many occasions for worship visual settings. Start gathering your items slowly. You do not have to spend a fortune on supplies. Many times you will be able to borrow items from team members or members of the congregation. The following is a list of basic supplies that you may wish to have on hand.

FABRIC

Build a collection of fabric in the colors of the Christian Year. Each fabric will have characteristics of color, texture, flexibility (the stiffness or suppleness of the fabric), and pattern. Divide the fabrics into the following categories:

- Rough textured fabrics, such as burlap, monk's cloth, some felts, canvas, wool, and chenille
- Smooth textured fabrics, such as silks, satins, most cottons, tulle, and lining fabric
- Specialty fabrics, such as netting, brocades, metallics, lace, and nylon organza

In general, stay away from print or striped fabrics. The designs dominate, and the items that are placed on them get lost in the patterns. Bold fabrics used in large quantities will take away from the effect of the display. Use bold stripes and patterns sparingly and only if they really are necessary for the theme.

Certain fabrics and patterns are identified with cultural or national groups, such as boldly colored

Kente cloth, Mexican fabrics with vivid stripes, and gently printed oriental fabrics. They are useful if they work with the theme of the worship service and the overall visual design. Note that the bolder the fabric, the larger the coordinating items. Also, the items should be solid in color so they do not compete with the fabric's pattern.

An investment in solid-colored cotton fabrics is a good place to start. Most plain cotton fabrics are 45 inches wide and sell by the yard. For example, you could purchase:

- Ten yards of purple cloth (for use during Advent and Lent)
- Ten yards of white fabric
- Eight yards each of black, red, and green cotton fabric

Cotton-polyester fabric resists wrinkles and drapes very nicely on the communion table. Prices on cotton-polyester and cotton fabrics in solid colors vary greatly, depending on the quality of the fabric. Most fabric stores sell basic apparel and quilting cotton solids at very reasonable prices. Always check the bargain fabric section for suitable cottons.

Burlap is another wonderful investment. The burlap most commonly available at fabric stores is a natural tan color and about 54 inches wide. The weave is close and the fabric is very stiff. The stiffness will soften with usage. Landscaper's burlap, which comes in fifty-foot rolls, is very rough in texture and has a more open weave. You may want to consider purchasing one or two rolls of landscaper's burlap for your Holy Hardware stash.

Silk linings in a variety of colors are wonderful for conveying a sense of flow. Silkene, a lining fabric, is excellent for water images. Satins, brocades, lace, tulle, nylon netting, and nylon organza all have special qualities that add interesting effects in visual designs and displays.

Are there any "fabric hounds" in your congregation? These people know where to get fabrics at the best price for the quality. They are a great resource for the visual artist.

ACRYLIC PAINTS

Acrylic paint (liquid rather than tube paints) is preferable to other types of paint because it dries quickly and can be removed from the brushes with soap and water. However, acrylics will dry on clothing and cannot be removed, so caution is recommended. Acrylic paints may be purchased in hobby and art stores, as well as at fabric and craft stores.

ROOM DARKENING "CANVAS"

Room darkening fabric is sold in home decorating stores, and it is used in many hotels as drapery liner. One side of the fabric is canvas and the other side is often a rubberized material. One of the best things about this fabric is the ease with which it takes paint. When the painting is dry, the art piece may be rolled up and stored, preferably in a tube of some kind. This makes for relatively easy storage if your space is limited. Generally this fabric comes in 54-inch-wide rolls, and you can cut it to any size. It does not unravel. If you want to make a hem or a casing for a rod (to hang a banner, for example), you can simply fold over the piece and fasten it with hot glue.

CANDLES AND HOLDERS

Tapers come in a variety of colors and heights. They can be purchased in quantity and are easily stored. Votive candles and holders also come in many colors and can lend a pleasing atmosphere to the worship display.

Pillar candles (two inches in diameter or wider) are often a better investment than tapers because they typically last longer. The problem with pillar candles is that they may begin to burn through their sides, with wax dripping down the candle. There is a unique solution to this problem. When the candle burns down approximately one inch, insert an Emkay votive candle. (Many religious supply houses sell Emkay inserts.) The inserts may be purchased in "burn hours," such as four-hour, six-hour, and eight-hour candles. The four-hour-burn Emkay candles are the smallest and fit neatly into the cavity of a pillar candle. When the inserts are no longer usable, simply discard them.

The plastic containers of the inserts do not heat up enough to adhere to the sides of the pillar candle. If you place tea lights or small votives in the pillar, they will stick to the candle, and you have to dig them out. You risk destroying the candle in the process.

Three-wick candles are interesting and can be used in many settings. Consider keeping two white ones in stock.

To keep wax off the surface of the display table, put a metal or ceramic holder under each candle. Pillar candles can be placed in large pedestal holders. Use the holders that work best with your design and display. For formal designs, shiny holders (made of glass, brass, or metals) are useful. For informal designs, wood, ceramic, or stone holders work well.

ROCKS, WOOD, SHELLS, AND SUCH

Rosemary Brown, author of *Visual Images for Worship*, delights in the wonderful world of rocks, wood, shells, and other "found" objects. These natural items can add a delightful quality to your visual displays.

Smooth, polished rocks may be purchased in quantity from most arts and crafts stores or aquarium shops. Rough rocks may be purchased from landscaping supply stores or gathered from your yard or garden. Large rocks are obviously very heavy and difficult to store. Although artificial "boulders" may be purchased at landscaping supply or hardware stores, they are expensive. Local theater groups often have "fake" large rocks and boulders you may borrow.

DOWELS AND PVC PIPE

Wood dowels are often used as rods for banners. PVC pipe, which can be purchased at hardware or building supply stores, can also be used. These pipes come in various diameters up to six inches. For lightweight fabrics, pipes one inch in diameter work well. For heavier fabrics, use two-inch pipes. If you are making a longer banner, you will want heavier pipe.

RISERS, EASELS, AND MUSIC STANDS

When designing a visual worship display, use "air space"—that is, create various levels or heights from the main horizontal surface; place items on these levels or "risers" to enable better viewing. All risers should be sturdy enough to safely hold the items that will be placed on them.

Risers may simply be stacked blocks of wood, sturdy cardboard boxes, or wooden boxes. In many of the *Praise Now! 2* displays, stacked blocks and smaller "shelves" were used. Often, a large riser was placed on the back of the table: twelve inches high, about six inches deep, and running the full length of the table. This riser is basically three pieces of wood screwed together.

Artist easels can create height, or they may be used for displaying paintings or icons on or near the displays. Tabletop easels may be used on the table itself. Floor models may be used to support paintings or, when covered with fabric, give additional height to the display. To give height to fabric, use music stands raised to the desired level.

PLANTS AND FRUIT (REAL AND ARTIFICIAL)

Although some people prefer to use real fruits, flowers, plants, vegetables, and grain in worship displays, many artificial products are preferable. Storage for these items is easy, there is no spoilage, and you can use them over and over again. Carefully chosen artificial bunches of grapes and other fruits, or flowers, vines and other greens (such as silk) look beautiful. Stay away from plastic flowers, however, as they do not look real.

If you want to use the "real thing" and have a limited budget, ask members of your congregation for help. They will likely be generous in loaning some of the above items for displays.

PAINTINGS, BANNERS, ICONS, SIGNS

Gather these items over a period of time. Make sure that they are large enough to be seen at a distance and that they pertain to the specific service for which you plan to use them.

Borrowing Items

If you borrow any items, take very good care of them. Label them in such a way that they may be returned quickly, accompanied with a note of appreciation. Many members of the congregation will be happy to loan items. As a way of saying "thanks" and acknowledging the donation, list in the bulletin (or on an insert) the names of persons who have loaned items for the day's visual display.

Some businesses, such as your local florist, may be willing to let you borrow specific items from them. Check around your area and see what you can find.

1. Mission Impossible?

(Advent)

(Most suitable for the Third Sunday of Advent)

Musical Invitation *(Worship music leaders may play/sing any of the songs listed below, or another appropriate selection.)*

Welcome
(Welcome the people. If this is the First Sunday of Advent, acknowledge the beginning of the season and give a brief description of Advent. See BOW, no. 238.)

Lighting the Advent Candle
(You may select a family or an individual to light the Advent candles and to offer the following.)

During Advent, we are invited to respond to
    God's call to us.
Today's Advent candle represents trust.
We will look at God's interaction with two men,
    Zechariah and Joseph,
each of whom trusted God in individual but strong
    ways.
Perhaps you will find that God is also calling to you.

(Candles are lit as the congregation sings the response.)

Sung Response: "Rejoice, Rejoice" (from "O Come, O Come, Emmanuel"), UMH, no. 211
(Sing refrain twice.) (See also MGB, WOW Christmas, and CC.)

Song: "Come, Thou Long-Expected Jesus," UMH, no. 196
(For a 1950s doo-wop arrangement of this hymn, see Resources below.)

Worship Focus
L: This is the time of waiting for the fulfillment of God's promise. Deliverance is offered for God's special people.
P: We don't see ourselves as anything special— we're just ordinary people.
L: On the contrary—God believes that you are special and God has a place for you in the healing of the world.
P: We're a little afraid of what might happen. We don't know what to say.

L: You don't have to say anything yet, just listen and follow. God will take care of you. You can rely on that!
P: Praise be to God for God's steadfast love for us. Amen.

Song: "The Steadfast Love of the Lord" by Edith McNeill (MGB, no. 247)
(Sing at least two times. If the song is new to the congregation, have the worship music leaders sing it once and then invite the congregation to join.)

Video Clip: *The Fellowship of the Ring*
    DVD, Disc 1:
    START—33:49. Frodo says to Gandalf, "Take it! Take it!" [the ring]
    STOP—35:36. Gandalf says to Frodo, "They [hobbits] can still surprise you."

In the film, *The Lord of the Rings: The Fellowship of the Ring*, Frodo Baggins is confronted with a dilemma. Upon the arrival of Gandalf, the wizard, and the disappearance of his uncle, Bilbo Baggins, Frodo is called to a task that will change his life radically. The ring of great power has been passed to him, but he must dispose of it in the fires of Mordor, the realm of evil. Feeling inadequate to the task, he seeks help from Gandalf, who reminds him that he, Frodo, is the only one who can safely dispose of this ring. He just has to have faith in himself and in his mission.

Song: "Cry of My Heart," TFWS, no. 2165 *(refrain, stanza 1, refrain) (Also found in DMC and WOW Green.)*

"The Story of Zechariah": Scripture Tableau (Luke 1:8-20)

(Three readers needed.)

Narrator: Luke 1:8-13*a*, 18*a*, 19*a*
Angel: Luke 1:13*b*-17, 19*b*-20
Zechariah: Luke 1:18*b*

Message Movers—Part 1
1. Zechariah was attentive to his duties in the Temple. He was a responsible member of the clergy.

2. The angel greeted Zechariah with the statement: "Do not be afraid," and the message that his wife will conceive and bear a son.

3. Zechariah "knows what he knows." ("She's too old to have a baby.") Zechariah listens to his fear and not to the faith that he has proclaimed.

4. The consequence of Zechariah's response is imposed silence—a time to think and reflect on what is about to happen.

Song: "Cry of My Heart," TFWS, no. 2165 *(refrain, stanza 2, refrain)*

"The Story of Joseph's Dream": Scripture Tableau (Matt. 1:18-25)
(Three readers needed; these may be the same persons who presented "The Story of Zechariah.")

> **Narrator:** Matt. 1:18-20*a*, 24-25
> **Angel:** Matt. 1:20*b*-23
> **Joseph:** (nonreading part)

Message Movers—Part 2

1. Joseph was confronted with a dilemma. Mary, his betrothed, was pregnant with a child that was not his—and her story of the child being the product of the Holy Spirit seemed implausible. What should he do? Conventional wisdom said to divorce her, but he was troubled by this. He would not divorce her publicly, for he did not want to disgrace her. This would be done in private, to spare her feelings and the honor of her family.

2. Again, an emissary of God intervenes with a message not to fear. What Mary had told him was true and he should honor her. His response was to follow the guidance of the angel.

3. Zechariah and Joseph were both encouraged to let go of their fear and believe in the power of God. Each responded individually: Zechariah questioned the possibilities; Joseph obeyed.

4. We are so content with our own knowledge that we are afraid to let go and let God work the miracles. We are challenged to let go of what we understand to be possible and to trust in God's word and will. When we quiet down, our fears are turned into faith as we let God's word and love for us enter in and transform our lives.

Song: "Lord, Have Mercy" by Steve Merkel *(worship music leaders)*
(See WA songbook and CD. Soloist sings the stanzas and worship music leaders sing the first two refrains. Invite the congregation to join in the singing of the last two refrains [measure 53 to the end]. If possible, use a violin or oboe for the solo instrumental part, or play the part on a MIDI keyboard patch and play the accompaniment on piano.)

Prayer Time
Sung Response: "Lord, Have Mercy" *(Congregation sings refrain twice.)*

Prayer Following the Prayer Time
You continually surprise us, Lord, with your presence and transforming love.
Keep us alert and awake to receive your gift of life, letting go of our fears.
Change us so that we may fully serve you in all that we do.
Help us to be the loving community that you intended, a community of peace. Amen.

Opportunities for Service

Offering/Closing Song: "Lord, Reign in Me" by Brenton Brown *(See DMC or WOW Green.)*

(Worship music leaders sing or play "Lord, Reign in Me" for the congregation. Once the offering is collected, invite the congregation to stand and sing the song.)

Sending Forth
Beloved friends, God is calling you into God's world.
Welcome the surprises that await you. Fear not.
Place your trust in God's steadfast love for you.
May the peace of God go with you always. Amen.

(Worship music leaders may play/sing "Lord, Reign in Me" or "The Steadfast Love of the Lord" as the congregation exits.)

Service 1. "Mission Impossible?" Visual Resources and Ideas

DESIGN CONCEPT

The scriptures center on God's call to two men, Zechariah and Joseph. Zechariah is a Temple priest; Joseph is a simple carpenter. In the visual display, Zechariah is represented by the scroll, the prayer shawl, and the burgundy silkene fabric. Joseph is represented by the burlap, wood pieces, and hand tools. The burgundy pillar candle represents God's call to the two men. Because this service occurs during Advent, we have placed the traditional Advent candles above the main display, surrounded by ivy.

DESIGN AND DISPLAY SUPPLIES AND RESOURCES

Structure

A riser the length of the table (approximately 66" x 12" x 6") was placed at the back of the table. Two smaller "risers" (wood blocks about five inches high) were placed on the table: one on the left side to support the items representing Zechariah, and the other on the right side to support the wood and tools representing Joseph.

Fabric

Purple or blue may be used in Advent. Drape ten yards of purple cotton (45 inches wide) across the table. Begin at the top and gradually drape the fabric back and forth until the entire table is covered. Leave enough fabric so that it "puddles" on the floor. This creates a fuller look and a softer line.

"Puddle" approximately three yards of burgundy silkene, representing Zechariah, on the left side of the table and drape over the side. "Puddle" approximately three yards of tight weave burlap, representing Joseph, on the right side of the table. The fabrics meet and overlap in the center of the table.

Candles

Use two 6-inch and two 8-inch purple pillar candles on the risers in place of the traditional round Advent wreath. If using blue fabric, also use blue candles. In the display, only three candles were lighted, suggesting the Third Sunday of Advent. Place a burgundy 6-inch pillar candle on the main level of the table to represent God's call to Zechariah and Joseph. It ties the design together.

Florals and Plants

Weave a long strand of large artificial ivy around the Advent candles to soften the look of the design. Ivy is one of the traditional plants used in Advent.

Other Items

Create the scroll for Zechariah by cutting two broomstick handles about fifteen inches long and attaching wood finials to either end. Spray paint them gold. Staple drapery lining to the wood handles and roll in scroll fashion. Place a clergy stole under the scroll to represent Zechariah's prayer shawl.

Place pieces of wood and wood hand tools on the burlap to represent Joseph. The wood pieces in front of the table give movement to the design and break the draped pattern created by the two fabrics.

SPECIAL NOTES

After the service, while the candles are still warm, pour the melted wax into a paper hot cup, and discard the cup once the wax has hardened. Try to avoid having the wax drip down the side of the candles. If some should drip down, carefully remove the drips with a razor blade, trying not to scratch the surface.

VISUAL RESOURCES

- Fabric: Burgundy silkene, purple cotton, tightly woven burlap, purchased at a local fabric store
- Artificial ivy: Borrowed from Nancy Townley's "Holy Hardware" supply
- Candles: Purchased at a local craft store
- Broomstick handles, wood pieces, and wood tools: Supplied by a member of the visual arts team
- Clergy stole: Supplied by Nancy Townley

WORSHIP RESOURCES

"Come, Thou Long-Expected Jesus," UMH, no. 196. Also available in a 1950s doo-wop arrangement by Nylea Butler-Moore. Contact Nylea Butler-Moore at nbmoosic@aol.com.

"Cry of My Heart," TFWS, no. 2165. See also DMC Songbook, p. 20 and CD, disc B; or WOW Green Songbook, p. 32 and CD, disc 2.

"Lord, Have Mercy," WA Songbook, p. 31 and CD; solo tracks available from Provident Music Distribution.

"O Come, O Come Emmanuel" ("Rejoice, Rejoice"), UMH, no. 211. See also MGB, no. 55; CC, no. 22; or WOW Christmas Songbook, p. 109 and CD.

"The Steadfast Love of the Lord," MGB, no. 247.

ADDITIONAL RESOURCES

"A Mighty Fortress Is Our God," MGB, no. 1.

"A Strange Way to Save the World," WOW Christmas Songbook, p. 92 and CD, red disc.

"For Certain," a song about Joseph and his dilemma regarding Mary, by Nylea L. Butler-Moore. Lead sheet available. Contact Nylea at nbmoosic@aol.com.

"Great Is Thy Faithfulness," MGB, no. 189.

"I Want to Follow You" by Cheri Keaggy from *There Is Joy in the Lord* CD (Sparrow). See also OGR, p. 103.

"Lord, I'm in Your Hands," MGB, no. 133.

"O Come, O Come, Emmanuel/God Rest Ye Merry, Gentlemen," CC, no. 22.

The Lord of the Rings: The Fellowship of the Ring. Tolkien Enterprises, New Line Productions, Inc. Available in DVD (widescreen version) or VHS format.

"The Power of Your Love," MGB, no. 157.

"Trust in the Lord" by Nylea L. Butler-Moore (Huey Lewis and the News style). Lead sheet available. Contact Nylea at nbmoosic@aol.com.

"Undivided Heart," MGB, no. 77.

"We Will Follow," CC, no. 59.

Mission Impossible?

Musical Invitation *(Worship Music Leaders)*

Welcome

Lighting the Advent Candle

Sung Response: "Rejoice, Rejoice" (from "O Come, O Come, Emmanuel"), 9th cent. Latin *(Sing refrain twice.)*

Song: "Come, Thou Long-Expected Jesus" by Charles Wesley

Worship Focus

L: This is the time of waiting for the fulfillment of God's promise. Deliverance is offered for God's special people.

P: We don't see ourselves as anything special—we're just ordinary people.

L: On the contrary—God believes that you are special and God has a place for you in the healing of the world.

P: We're a little afraid of what might happen. We don't know what to say.

L: You don't have to say anything yet, just listen and follow. God will take care of you. You can rely on that!

P: Praise be to God for God's steadfast love for us. Amen.

Song: "The Steadfast Love of the Lord" by Edith McNeill

Video Clip from *The Fellowship of the Ring*

Song: "Cry of My Heart" by Terry Butler *(Refrain, Stanza 1, Refrain)*

"The Story of Zechariah" (Luke 1:8-20)

Message—Part 1

Song: "Cry of My Heart" by Terry Butler *(Refrain, Stanza 2, Refrain)*

"The Story of Joseph's Dream" (Matt. 1:18-25)

Message—Part 2

Song: "Lord, Have Mercy" by Steve Merkel *(Worship Music Leaders)*

Prayer Time
   Sung Response: "Lord, Have Mercy" *(Sing refrain twice.)*
   Prayer Following the Prayer Time

Opportunities for Service

Offering/Closing Song: "Lord, Reign in Me" by Brenton Brown

Sending Forth

God chooses the most desirable people to fulfill God's will

Luke 1:26-39
Luke 2:8-20

2. You Talkin' to Me?

(Advent)
(Most suitable for the Fourth Sunday of Advent)

Musical Invitation *(Worship music leaders may play/sing any of the songs listed below, or an appropriate selection of their choosing.)*

Greeting and Opportunities for Service

Songs: "Come, Now Is the Time to Worship" by Brian Doerksen
(See DMC, WOW Blue, or iWOR.)

"You Are Holy (Prince of Peace)" by Mark Imboden and Tammi Rhoton
(See WA or iWOR.)

Lighting the Advent Candle
(You may select a family or an individual to light the Advent candles and to offer the following.)

Today we light the fourth Advent candle, which represents obedience.
We will look at God's interaction with Mary and the shepherds.
The eyes of Mary and the shepherds were opened as they saw God's glory and responded in obedience to God's Word.
Perhaps God is calling you to do something.

(Candles are lit as the congregation sings the response.)

Sung Response: "Rejoice, Rejoice" (from "O Come, O Come, Emmanuel"), UMH, no. 211
(Sing refrain twice.) (See also MGB, WOW Christmas, and CC.)

Worship Focus

Call to Worship
L: Are you ready to receive good news?
P: We surely are! There's too much bad news in our world.
L: God has a special gift for you.
P: For us? What have we ever done that God should give us a gift?
L: Nothing. God just wants you to know how much you are loved.

P: Where is this gift of love?
L: Look at the cradle, the cross, and in your hearts. God is speaking God's word of love to you right now.

Song: "Rise Up, Shepherd, and Follow," TFWS, no. 2096
(If you have an interpretative dance group, consider developing choreography to accompany the song. See Worship Resources below for information on Mark Hayes's swing arrangement of this song.)

Message Movers—Part 1
(During the message, you may wish to project a portion of the scripture using transparencies, PowerPoint or Media Shout, or other slide presentation software. This visual presentation may include graphics that relate to the main points. See below for ideas.)

Very few of us expect angelic visitations. We are no different in that regard from Mary, the young woman in Nazareth or the third-shift shepherds on the hillsides. Nothing in Mary's young life led her to believe that God would select her as the mother of the Messiah. Nothing in the experiences of the shepherds led them to believe that they would be the first to receive the good news of Messiah's birth.

The angelic appearance is to Mary, a young girl of an average working-class family. The initial greeting, "Greetings, O favored one!" perplexes Mary and she is afraid. *(You may project Luke 1:28b here.)*

The angel says, "Do not be afraid," and offers her the good news that she has been chosen to bear the Messiah.

Mary's question is much like ours would be: "Who, me?"

Rather than censuring Mary, the angel reassures her that it is part of God's plan. *(You may project Luke 1:38 here.)*

We would probably have the same reaction as Mary. Why would God choose us to be part of God's plan? We are not powerful, wonderful, or truly wise. We're just average folk. Harry Potter could certainly identify with this problem. As far as he knew he was just an average boy. Nothing could be further from the truth.

**Video Clip from *Harry Potter and the Sorcerer's Stone*
DVD, Disc 1:** START—14:46 (portion of scene 4)
STOP—15:26

In the film, *Harry Potter and the Sorcerer's Stone*, Harry Potter's unique heritage has been carefully and intentionally kept from him. In this scene, Hagrid, the keeper of keys and grounds at Hogwarts School, informs Harry that he is a wizard ("and a thumpin' good one, I'll wager"). Harry's initial reaction is disbelief. ("I can't be a wizard. I'm Harry, just Harry.") Harry is awestruck, but trusts in Hagrid's word.

Message Movers—Part 2

Third-shift shepherds are the lowest of the low. They had no power or prestige. Often they were the "throw-away" people. Like Harry Potter, the shepherds never expected anything special to happen to them. Yet, like Harry Potter, God had a surprise in store.

One night on a lonely hillside, the shepherds witnessed a sky ablaze with the presence of angelic messengers, proclaiming that God's Son had been born in Bethlehem. This Son of God was given for them. And they were filled with fear.

They were the first to receive the news, not the mighty and powerful people. Third-shift shepherds were told that God had done a mighty thing for all of humankind.

Like the shepherds, we are given the good news of Messiah's birth. Like the shepherds, we are raised up and given hope; we are beloved of God. Those who least expect God's love are often most surprised by it. Fear is turned into faith as we rejoice in Emmanuel, "God with *us*." With incredible wisdom, God chooses those who feel like the most unlikely ones to bear the witness to God's great love. Our fear is turned into faith as we recognize that God will use us to be bearers of hope. Like Mary, our souls give glory to God because God has done great things for us.

Song: "My Soul Gives Glory to My God," UMH, no. 198 (Luke 1:46-55)

Prayer Time
Intercessions for individuals/situations
Sung Response: "Lord, Have Mercy" by Steve Merkel *(Two refrains only)* (See WA.)
Prayers for the world and for our enlightenment and service in that world

Offering: "Breath of Heaven" by Chris Eaton and Amy Grant

(Worship music leaders featuring a soloist; see WOW Christmas.)

Sending Forth Prayer
Gentle God, no one stands outside your presence.
As you came to Mary with the invitation to be the
        Mother of Christ,
you have come to us with your invitation of healing
        that we might bear the good news to others.
As you visited the shepherds on the dark night so
        long ago,
you visit our darkness with your light.
Free us to be your people,
        that we may live our lives for you. Amen.

Closing Song: "You Are Holy (Prince of Peace)" by Mark Imboden and Tammi Rhoton
(Use measure 21 to the end, with the congregation singing part 2.)

(Worship music leaders may play/sing "You Are Holy" as the congregation exits.)

Service 2: "You Talkin' to Me?" Visual Resources and Ideas

DESIGN CONCEPT

The scripture focuses on God's call to Mary and the announcement of the good news to the shepherds. Keep the visual theme simple.

DESIGN AND DISPLAY SUPPLIES AND RESOURCES

Structure

Use the long table riser from Service 1, along with three block risers under the purple fabric on the main level of the table. They support one angel and two shepherds.

Fabric

Cover the table and long riser with ten yards of purple cotton fabric. "Puddle" the fabric on the floor to soften the line and create a sense of fullness to the design. Drape eight yards of light blue netting across the back of the main level of the table to symbolize Mary, giving it an ethereal look. Cover the base of the large-leafed plant with burgundy silkene fabric.

Candles

Place the Advent candles (two 6-inch and two 8-inch purple pillar candles) on the top of the long table riser. Blue is the alternate color for Advent. If you are using blue, purchase blue pillar candles to coordinate with the fabric.

Florals and Plants

Weave a long strand of artificial ivy between the candles on the table riser. Place a large-leafed plant on the floor in front of the table to anchor and soften the line at the base of the table.

Other Items

Position two angels in the design: one on the upper left portion of the table riser between the 6-inch and 8-inch purple pillar candles and the other on top of a 4-inch block riser, which is under the purple cloth. Place two shepherds on top of 2-inch block risers, which are under the purple cloth. Place the other shepherds and sheep on the main level of the table.

SPECIAL NOTES

Our local florist was a wonderful resource for borrowed plants. There may be people in your congregation who have such wonderful plants and would be willing to lend them to you for the worship service. If you borrow anything from anyone, place a small tag on the item listing the name of the owner, so it may be returned promptly. Keep a record of all the items borrowed.

Following the worship service while the candles are still warm, pour the melted wax into a paper hot cup and discard the cup once the wax has hardened. Scrape any drips that occur on the candle very carefully from the surface of the candle, taking care not to scratch the candle surface.

VISUAL RESOURCES

- Fabric: Purple cotton fabric (ten yards), light blue netting (ten yards) and burgundy silkene (suit lining), purchased in a local fabric store
- Artificial ivy: Borrowed from Nancy Townley's "Holy Hardware" supply
- Large-leafed plant: Borrowed from Bud's Florist and Greenhouse
- Shepherds: On loan from St. Paul's UMC, Castleton, NY
- Angels: Borrowed from a personal collection

WORSHIP RESOURCES

"Breath of Heaven (Mary's Song)," WOW Christmas Songbook, p. 100 and CD, red disc.

"Come, Now Is the Time to Worship," DMC Songbook, p. 15 and CD, disc B. See also WOW Blue Songbook, p. 31 and CD, blue disc; or iWOR Songbook and CD set.

Harry Potter and the Sorcerer's Stone. Warner Brothers Home Video. Available in DVD or VHS format. For more information, visit www.harrypotter.com.

"Lord, Have Mercy," WA Songbook, p. 31 and CD.

"My Soul Gives Glory to My God," UMH, no. 198.

"O Come, O Come Emmanuel" ("Rejoice, Rejoice"), UMH, no. 211. See also MGB, no. 55; CC, no. 22; or WOW Christmas Songbook, p. 109 and CD, red disc.

"Rise Up, Shepherd, and Follow," TFWS, no. 2096. Arranged in a swing style by Mark Hayes, in a variety of voicings from Alfred Publishing Company, Inc. CD and instrumental parts also available.

"You Are Holy (Prince of Peace)," WA Songbook, p. 67 and CD. See also iWOR, DVD "D"; solo tracks available from Praise Hymn Soundtracks.

ADDITIONAL RESOURCES

"Ave Maria," WOW Christmas songbook, p. 145 and CD, red disc.

"Carol of the Epiphany," TFWS, no. 2094

"Do You Hear What I Hear?" WOW Christmas Songbook, p. 153 and CD, gold disc.

"He Is Able," MGB, no. 192.

"Immanuel," OGR, p. 112.

"Jesus, Come/Emmanuel," CC, no. 23.

"Like a Rose in Winter," CC, no. 24.

"Mary, Did You Know?" WOW Christmas Songbook, p. 130 and CD, red disc. See also Kathy Mattea, *Good News* (Hal Leonard Corporation), songbook and CD; solo tracks available from Praise Hymn Soundtracks.

You Talkin' to Me?

Musical Invitation *(Worship Music Team)*

Greeting and Opportunities for Service

Songs: "Come, Now Is the Time to Worship" by Brian Doerksen
"You Are Holy (Prince of Peace)" by Mark Imboden and Tammi Rhoton

Lighting the Advent Candle

Sung Response: "Rejoice, Rejoice" (from "O Come, O Come, Emmanuel"), 9th cent. Latin *(Sing refrain twice.)*

Worship Focus

Call to Worship
L: Are you ready to receive good news?
P: We surely are! There's too much bad news in our world.
L: God has a special gift for you.
P: For us? What have we ever done that God should give us a gift?
L: Nothing. God just wants you to know how much you are loved.
P: Where is this gift of love?
L: Look at the cradle, the cross, and in your hearts.
    God is speaking God's word of love to you right now.

Song: "Rise Up, Shepherd, and Follow" *(traditional spiritual)*

Message—Part 1

Video Clip from *Harry Potter and the Sorcerer's Stone*

Message—Part 2

Song: "My Soul Gives Glory to My God" by Miriam Therese Winter

Prayer Time
    Intercessions for individuals/situations
    Sung Response: "Lord, Have Mercy" by Steve Merkel *(two refrains only)*
    Prayers for the World

Offering: "Breath of Heaven (Mary's Song)" by Chris Eaton and Amy Grant *(Worship Music Leaders)*

Sending Forth Prayer

Closing Song: "You Are Holy (Prince of Peace)" by Mark Imboden and Tammi Rhoton

3. Heaven Can't Wait

(Christmas Eve or Christmas Day)

Musical Invitation: "Emmanuel" by Michael W. Smith (*Worship Music Leaders*) (*See WOW Christmas.*)

Call to Worship
L: Darkness is banished;
P: God's light has come.
L: Silence is over;
P: God's Word has come.
L: Fear is driven out;
P: God's love is here!

Lighting the Advent Candles and the Christ Candle
(*You may select a family or an individual to light the Advent candles and to offer the following.*)

Rejoice, dear friends!
We celebrate this eve/day by lighting
    all the Advent candles and the Christ candle.
The world, which once dwelled in darkness,
    now receives the Light of God's love.
The Love of God comes to dwell with us—
    Emmanuel.
The darkness is banished! Rejoice!

(*Candles are lit as the congregation sings the response.*)

Sung Response: "Rejoice, Rejoice" (from "O Come, O Come, Emmanuel"), UMH, no. 211
(*Sing refrain twice using the following words.*)

"Rejoice! Rejoice! Emmanuel has come to thee, O Israel."

(*See also MGB, CC, and WOW Christmas.*)

Opening Prayer
God of prophets and average people,
    with great wonder and delight,
We open our hearts to hear your Good News.
We stand on tiptoes to receive the blessings,
    which you have for us this day/night.
Bring your transforming light to us and empower us
    to be your faithful children in this world.
Cause us to shout the words of hope and joy
    in the midst of darkness. Amen.

Song: "O Come, All Ye Faithful," UMH, no. 234
(*Stanzas 1, 3, and 6*) (*See MGB and WOW Christmas for setting of this hymn. For an upbeat version of this carol, see Additional Resources below.*)

Offering
(*Use this time to feature special music by the children's choir, youth choir, or other ensemble.*)

"Christmas Presence" (*Skit*)
(*Four nongender-specific characters.*)

PERSON 1: I love Christmas! All the decorations, the music, the parties! Everyone seems happier during this time of year. People smile at one another—they're just like little children, waiting for Santa, stringing popcorn garlands. So many places to go and so many people to see! We sent out more Christmas cards than ever before and received more, let me tell you. Oh, it's so wonderful!

VOICE: In the beginning was the Word, and the Word was with God.

PERSON 2: Are you kidding? Lord, I hate this time of year! I can't wait until Christmas is over! Everyone expects so much. I had to address all the Christmas cards, do all the shopping, and ship all the packages to relatives. Then there was the obligatory party for the coworkers, and all the places I had to cart the kids. Relatives showed up, the house was a wreck, there wasn't enough food for everyone.

VOICE: And the Word became flesh and dwelled among us.

PERSON 3: Society puts a lot of pressures on us at Christmas time. It is so easy to become over-whelmed, and then we miss the whole point of the season. "Where is the hope? Where is the peace that will make this life complete for every man, woman, boy, and girl, looking for heaven in the real world?"

VOICE: And the time came when she should be delivered. And she gave birth to her firstborn son and laid him in a manger, because there was no room for them in the inn.

(Begin playing the introduction to "The Virgin Mary Had a Baby Boy" at the beginning of the previous line. As the line is completed, have bearers bring forward a crèche, the figures of the Holy Family, the shepherds, and various animals, and angels. Place the crèche in the center of the communion table toward the back and place the figures in appropriate stances in and beside the crèche. Place a collection of votive candles on stands in front and to the right and left of the table covered with a white cloth.)

Song: "The Virgin Mary Had a Baby Boy," TFWS, no. 2098
(If possible, use a steel drum or other Caribbean-sounding setting on your MIDI keyboard. Consider using flute to play the top notes of the introduction and the ending, with occasional obbligato improvisation during some of the verses.)

Message Movers
(Read John 1:1-14. Consider showing the scripture on transparencies or slides.)

In the very beginning, God loved the world into being. All creation was blessed. Freedom of human beings led to some unique and destructive consequences. Too often people chose to follow their own way rather than to rely on God. God seemed to take a back seat or to be relegated to being a distant, judgmental rule-giver.

Again God offered love in the words of prophets, only to be rejected. God's Word became flesh and blood and dwells with us—fully identifying with our joys and sorrows.

Song: "Heaven in the Real World" by Steven Curtis Chapman.

(See Heaven in the Real World CD, Steven Curtis Chapman.)

(Worship music leaders, or play the CD recording accompanied by a graphic presentation you create.)

If we were to choose how "God with us" would come into the world, we would likely place him in a wealthy, secure environment. But God's Son would be born to a poor family. Joseph, a poor carpenter, takes his wife, Mary, to Bethlehem to register for the census, only to find that there is no place for them to stay. No relatives welcomed the weary couple. The rule of hospitality had been stretched to breaking, and no inn had room to house them. The stable, a place for housing animals, was the only available shelter. We have romanticized the scene with the lovely, demure Mary giving birth in the sanitary conditions of a make-believe stable and placing her child in an empty feed trough.

But God comes to us in the real world—not in a nice story for us to romanticize and then ignore. God comes as flesh and blood to dwell with us, where we are, in the conditions of our lives as imperfect as they are. God comes to us in love and compassion. The only preparation we need is to say "Yes" to God and to receive the Son with great joy and humility.

Song: "What Child Is This," UMH, no. 219
(Consider using guitar only, or flute and guitar.)

(See MGB and WOW Christmas for settings of this hymn.)

Prayer Time
Sung Response: "O Little Town of Bethlehem," UMH, no. 230 *(Stanza 4)*

(See MGB and WOW Christmas for settings of this hymn.)

Christmas Blessing
Heaven has come to earth!
God has made God's home with us
in the infant Savior Christ.
We rejoice in the light.
We celebrate the Word made flesh—Jesus.
May joy and peace reign in our hearts
as we celebrate God's Word dwelling among
us as light and love. Amen.

Closing Song: "Joy to the World," UMH, no. 246
(Stanzas 1, 2, and 4)

(See MGB and WOW Christmas for settings of this hymn.)

(Worship music leaders may play "Joy to the World" or other Christmas selection as the congregation exits.)

Service 3. "Heaven Can't Wait" Visual Resources and Ideas

DESIGN CONCEPT
Keeping with the traditional presentation of the Holy Family (or the Nativity), configure the table to reflect the heavenly scene. The circle of white netting suggests the embrace of God around the Nativity of God's Son.

DESIGN AND DISPLAY SUPPLIES AND RESOURCES

Structure
The long table riser (66" x 12" x 6") used in Services 1 and 2 is used again at the back of the table. Place two 2-inch risers under two of the white candles on the main level of the table. Place a piece of wood (6" x 2" x 6") under the purple fabric to raise the crèche scene slightly above table level.

Fabric

The ten-yard piece of purple cotton, which was used in the previous Advent scenes, remains on the table. Drape white netting (ten yards) behind the Nativity, around the candles, and down the sides of the table. Bring it around the front of the table and "bunch it up" around the large plant.

Candles

On the table riser, continue to use two 6-inch and two 8-inch purple pillar candles, and one 10-inch white pillar candle for the Christ candle. On the main level of the table use four 6-inch white pillar candles (place two on low block risers).

Florals and Plants

Put a long, large-leafed artificial ivy vine on the top riser around the candles. In front of the table, position the large-leafed plant to anchor the scene.

Other Items

The angel figures, which were used in the second Advent service above, are placed on each end of the top table riser. Center the stable and the Holy Family on the table and elevate the stable. Place straw in the stable and outside around the shepherds and sheep. Put the shepherds and the sheep to the right and left of the stable and slightly forward.

SPECIAL NOTES

Following the worship service, while the candles are still warm, pour the melted wax from the candles into a paper hot cup. This will keep it from building up within the candle. When the candles have burned down inside about one to two inches, insert a small Emkay brand votive candle. This will maintain the integrity of the candles so they can be used for many years.

Wrap the candles individually in tissue paper and store them in a cool, dry place. For the best storage, place the candles in boxes with dividers, such as those for bottles or jars. Mark on the outside of the box exactly what candles are in it. Carefully fold the purple fabric and netting and store in a plastic or cardboard bin. The artificial ivy may be stored in a large plastic bin. Always place a label on the front of containers to indicate the contents. Repack any borrowed items and return to the donor with a note of thanks.

VISUAL RESOURCES

- Fabric: Purple cotton and white netting, purchased from a local fabric store
- Large plant: Borrowed from Bud's Florist and Greenhouses
- Artificial ivy: Borrowed from Nancy Townley's "Holy Hardware" supply
- Nativity set and angels: Borrowed from Barbara and Jerry Popp, members of the visual arts team
- Candles: Purchased from a local craft store

WORSHIP RESOURCES

"Emmanuel," WOW Christmas Songbook, p. 23 and CD, red disc.

"Heaven in the Real World," Steven Curtis Chapman, *Heaven in the Real World* CD (Sparrow). Songbook available for piano and vocal, with guitar chords (Hal Leonard).

"Joy to the World," UMH, no. 246. See also MGB, no. 47 or CC, no. 31.

"O Come, All Ye Faithful," UMH, no. 234. See also MGB, no. 138 or WOW Christmas Songbook, p. 247 and CD, gold disc.

"O Come, O Come Emmanuel" ("Rejoice, Rejoice"), UMH, no. 211. See also MGB, no. 55; CC, no. 22; or WOW Christmas Songbook, p. 109 and CD, red disc.

"O Little Town of Bethlehem," UMH, no. 230. See also MGB, no. 57; CC, no, 26; or WOW Christmas Songbook, p. 229 and CD, gold disc.

"The Virgin Mary Had a Baby Boy," TFWS, no. 2098.

"What Child Is This," UMH, no. 219. See also MGB, no. 81 or WOW Christmas Songbook, p. 177 and CD, gold disc.

ADDITIONAL RESOURCES

"In the Bleak Midwinter," text by Christina G. Rossetti, music by Nylea L. Butler-Moore. In a Latin style, lead sheet available. For information, contact Nylea at nbmoosic@aol.com.

"O Come, All Ye Faithful," upbeat arrangement in a Beatles style, by Pete Brosnan. Lead sheet available. For information, contact Nylea Butler-Moore at nbmoosic@aol.com.

Heaven Can't Wait

Musical Invitation: "Emmanuel" by Michael W. Smith *(Worship Music Leaders)*

Call to Worship
L: Darkness is banished;
P: God's light has come.
L: Silence is over;
P: God's Word has come.
L: Fear is driven out;
P: God's love is here!

Lighting the Advent Candles and the Christ Candle

    Sung Response: "Rejoice, Rejoice" (from "O Come, O Come, Emmanuel"), 9th cent. Latin *(Sing refrain twice using the following words.)*

    "Rejoice! Rejoice! Emmanuel has come to thee, O Israel."

Opening Prayer

Song: "O Come, All Ye Faithful" by John F. Wade *(Stanzas 1, 3, and 6)*

Offering *(Special Music)*

"Christmas Presence" *(Skit)*

Song: "The Virgin Mary Had a Baby Boy" *(West Indian carol)*

Message
    Song: "Heaven in the Real World" by Steven Curtis Chapman *(Worship Music Leaders or CD)*

Song: "What Child Is This" by William C. Dix

Prayer Time
    Sung Response: "O Little Town of Bethlehem" by Phillips Brooks *(Stanza 4)*

Christmas Blessing

Closing Song: "Joy to the World" by Isaac Watts *(Stanzas 1, 2, and 4)*

Ridding ourselves of obstacles that block God's call

Jeremiah 29:13-14
Matthew 7:7-11

4. Clearing the Clutter
(Epiphany)

Musical Invitation *(Worship Music Leaders or CD)*

(Encourage the people to be in an attitude of quiet meditation as they enter the worship space. Play soothing instrumental music. Any of the selections from the Communion with God *CD would work well; see Additional Resources below for information. You could create an accompanying slide presentation if desired. Visuals could include pictures of the ocean, mountains, meadows, and so on.)*

Song: "I Choose You" by Maureen Pranghofer *(See CC.)*
"In the Secret" by Andy Park *(See DMC and WOW Orange.)*

(Use this format for "In the Secret": stanza 1, refrain, stanza 2, refrain, stanza 1, refrain, refrain. Play the stanzas in a more subdued feel and build in the refrains.)

Worship Focus: *(Worship Leader)*
Our worship today will focus on clearing away the clutter from our lives.
Through periods of quiet and meditative reflection, we hope you will relax and let God help you move through the clutter of living to a place of peace.

Song: "Sanctuary," TFWS, no. 2164 *(Sing twice.)*

Drama: "Talking at God" by Jay Huguely *(See Worship Resources below for ordering information.)*

(Synopsis: A person at prayer talks at God rather than listens to God. For two actors, "Gordon" and "God"; "God" could be a male or female. Running time is approximately six minutes. The person who plays "God" may also play the "Voice" of God in the Interrupted Message below.)

Song: "Come and Find the Quiet Center," TFWS, no. 2128

Congregational Scripture Reading: Jeremiah 29:13-14*a*
When you search for me
you will find me;
If you seek me with all your heart,
I will let you find me, says the Lord.

(Consider superimposing this text over a serene landscape scene, or other soothing graphic. The keyboard player may softly continue playing "Come and Find the Quiet Center" or other music as the congregation reads the scripture.)

Interrupted Message

(This message may be presented as a type of drama between the speaker and the offstage voice of "God." The Voice may be read live, using a lapel or cordless microphone, or it may be prerecorded. Add more to the main part of the "message" if you desire, but recite the Voice part as written. The last sentence of each section is the cue for the Voice response.)

SPEAKER: We long to be connected to others. Many of us spend hours on the Internet, gathering information, making contacts, researching, and inhabiting chat rooms. For some, the Internet and the solitary confinement of their own rooms offer a virtual life. The constant use of the cell phone is endemic in our society. In just about every setting, you can hear the ring of cell phones: when people are driving, when they're sitting in airports, in schools, at work, at the grocery store, in restaurants. People have the cell phone glued to their ears, and scientists claim that the once neglected thumb is becoming a mighty digit from all the cell phone dialing. We have a desperate need for contact. The popularity of chat phone lines speaks to the loneliness in people's lives.

VOICE: "Can you hear me now?"

SPEAKER: We continue to seek, ask, and knock. We want to find people we can trust, who will befriend us, who will care about us, just as we are. We seek the God of Abraham, Jacob, and Isaac; the God of Jesus; the God of abundant compassion and presence. When the answers to our questions and our prayers are not readily available, we think that God has moved away. A sign on a Pentecostal church reads: "Does God seem distant? Who do you think moved?"

VOICE: "Can you hear me now?"

SPEAKER: We search, only to discover the clutter that we have poured into our lives. Navigating through this clutter is often difficult. God gets lost in the mess of our daily living, in the struggles that present themselves to us as opportunities or duties, in questions of security, finances, and relationships.

VOICE: "Can you hear me now?"

SPEAKER: We have a need to sort out our spiritual clutter—a need to clear the way so we can hear and recognize God's loving call.

VOICE: "Can you hear me now? Good! There was static on the line, but it's going away. How are you? It's been a long time since we've talked. I've tried to get you several times, but your line has been busy. I have call-waiting. It's great, you know. Even though I'm busy on one call, I always know when another call is coming in. The other feature I have is Caller ID, so I always know when you're calling. Perhaps you might consider getting Caller ID and call-waiting so you will know when I'm calling. What do you think? Well, I'll let you go now. I know how busy you are. But remember that I love you and always look forward to our chats."

SPEAKER: There will always be spiritual clutter, but we are called to pick through it. We are called to clear a path to the door through which God's Spirit will ask, knock, seek, and enter. Then, we will truly be found by God.

VOICE: "Can you hear me now?"

Song: "Seek Ye First," UMH, no. 405 *(See also WOW Green.)*

(Consider playing this song with a Reggae or Caribbean feel.)

Prayer Time

(Joys and concerns may be lifted up. Graphics and/or captions may be used to help to lead the congregants in their prayers. Be sure to provide some quiet time, without music, between each prayer concern—in the style of a guided meditation. At the end of prayer time, sing the following response.)

Sung Response: "Be Still and Know that I Am God," TFWS, no. 2057

Offering: "Be Still and Know" by Steven Curtis Chapman

(This may be a presentation piece, or you may play the CD recording.)

Opportunities for Service

Closing Song: "The Summons," TFWS, no. 2130
(Stanzas 1, 4, and 5)

(Consider using a harp and flute accompaniment. If these instruments aren't available, use MIDI keyboard patches, or acoustic guitar.)

Sending Forth Prayer

God, you continue to call us
and we have to decide whether or not to answer your call.
Help us to respond to you amidst the clutter in our lives.
Keep calling us. Amen.

(Worship music leaders may play "The Summons" as the congregation exits.)

Service 4. "Clearing the Clutter" Visual Resources and Ideas

DESIGN CONCEPT

As you think about the theme, discuss the many ways in which things get in our way of paying attention to God's call. Some people spend many, many hours on the computer, surfing the web or playing games. Others are consumed by schedules and calendars, by studies, or by letters and advertising that claim their time and interest. The Bible on the table reminds us to take time to listen for God's Word for us. The candle is symbolic of the light of God's spirit offered to us. Green is the traditional color for the season of Epiphany. Consider using a draping of tea-dyed muslin fabric to create interest and pattern.

DESIGN AND DISPLAY SUPPLIES AND RESOURCES

Structure

Use the long table riser at the back of the table. Place a 4-inch block of wood under the Bible to hold it at an angle. On the back riser, rest the basket with the letters and advertisements spilling from it. Place a milk crate in front of the table and cover it with the green cloth that "puddles" around the base, softening the lines. Lean a newspaper against the crate.

Fabric

Drape ten yards of green cotton fabric over the back table riser and across the table, bringing it to the front so that you can put it over the milk crate. Drape eight yards of tea-dyed muslin from the back top riser, down onto the main level of the table and across the table to the right side.

Candles

Only one candle is used in this setting, a burgundy six-inch pillar candle for contrast.

Florals and Plants

We were able to borrow many plants from a very generous florist. There are rubber tree plants on the top riser and on the main table level. On either side in plant stands we placed potted palms. In front of the palm on the right we used an artificial hydrangea plant (burgundy and white) to bring color to the side of the display. On the left side of the table, we used a large jade plant. We used two spiky plants in front of each corner of the table and placed the green fabric around their bases.

Other Items

Place a date book and a cellular phone on the top riser, as well as a series of books. Position the basket with the letters on the main level facing the right of the table. The large Holy Bible should be on the left side of the table. Put a laptop computer on the milk crate in front of the table, and lean a local newspaper against the crate.

SPECIAL NOTES

As with all things that are borrowed, carefully label them and be sure that they are returned promptly to their owners. Fold the fabric and store for future use.

VISUAL RESOURCES

• Fabric: Ten yards of green cotton and eight yards of tea-dyed muslin, purchased at a local fabric store
• Plants: Most borrowed from Bud's Florist and Greenhouse
• Jade plant and newspaper: Borrowed from Barbara and Jerry Popp, members of the visual arts team
• Candle: Purchased from a local craft store
• Laptop computer, date book and cellular phone: Borrowed from Lesley Leonard, member of the visual arts team
• Books and basket of mail: From Nancy Townley's office

WORSHIP RESOURCES

"Be Still and Know," Steven Curtis Chapman, *Speechless* songbook (Hal Leonard Corporation), p. 106; CD and solo tracks available from Sparrow Records. Visit www.scchapman.com for more information.

"Be Still and Know that I Am God," TFWS, no. 2057.

"Come and Find the Quiet Center," TFWS, no. 2128.

"I Choose You," CC songbook, no. 61 and CD.

"In the Secret," DMC songbook, p. 47 and CD, disc B. See also WOW Orange songbook, p. 103 and CD, orange disc. Solo tracks available from Praise Hymn Soundtracks.

"Sanctuary," TFWS, no. 2164.

"Seek Ye First," UMH, no. 405. See also WOW Green songbook, p. 110 and CD, disc 2.

"Talking at God," drama by Jay Huguely. Contact Jay Huguely at umcv@umcv.org.

"The Summons," TFWS, no. 2130.

ADDITIONAL RESOURCES

"Be Thou My Vision," CC, no. 13. See also Fernando Ortega, *Hymns of Worship* (Curb Records). For more information, visit www.fernandoortega.com.

"Come, Walk Beside Still Waters," CC, no. 40.

Communion with God, a Windham Hill Collection CD. For more information, visit www.windham.com.

"Fields of Plenty/Be Still My Soul," Amy Grant, *Legacy, Hymns of Faith*. Songbook and CD available from Word Records. (This cut would work nicely at the end of prayer time.) For more information, visit www.amygrant.com.

"God Be in My Head," CC, no. 75.

"Jesus, Draw Me Close," TFWS, no. 2159. See also WOW Green songbook, p. 90 and CD, disc 2.

"My One Thing," Rich Mullins, *Songs* (Hal Leonard Corporation). CD available from Reunion Records.

Prayers in UMH: "Finding Rest in God," no. 423; "Prayer for a New Heart," no. 392; "For Direction," no. 705.

"Serenity," UMH, no. 499. (Text only; could be used during prayer time.)

"Still Waters," MGB, no. 242.

"The Quiet Whisper of God" by J. Eric Schmidt, suitable for a soloist, small ensemble, or congregation, published in *Church Music Workshop* magazine, vol. 14.2 (Abingdon Press). For information, contact Debi Tyree at dtyree@umpublishing.org.

"Unashamed Love," WOW Green songbook, p. 163 and CD, disc 1.

"Walk with Me" Caedmon's Call, *Back Home* CD (Essential Records). For more information, visit www.caedmonscall.com.

"You've Searched Me," David Haas, *You Are Mine, Vol. 2* (GIA Publications, Inc.). Available in CD or cassette format.

Clearing the Clutter

Musical Invitation *(Worship Music Leaders or CD)*

Songs: "I Choose You" by Maureen Pranghofer
"In the Secret" by Andy Park

Worship Focus

Song: "Sanctuary" by John Thompson *(Sing twice.)*

Drama: "Talking at God" by Jay Huguely

Song: "Come and Find the Quiet Center" by Shirley Erena Murray

Congregational Scripture Reading: Jeremiah 29:13-14*a*

> When you search for me
>   you will find me;
> If you seek me with all your heart,
>   I will let you find me, says the Lord.

"Interrupted" Message

Song: "Seek Ye First" by Karen Lafferty

Prayer Time
Sung Response: "Be Still and Know that I Am God" by John Bell

Offering: "Be Still and Know" by Steven Curtis Chapman

Opportunities for Service

Closing Song: "The Summons" by John Bell *(Stanzas 1, 4, and 5)*

Sending Forth Prayer

5. Heart Vision

(Transfiguration Sunday)

Musical Invitation (*Worship Music Leaders*)

(*Worship music leaders may play/sing any of the songs listed below, or an appropriate selection of their choosing. The players in the skit interrupt the music presentation. The keyboardist could then play a short segue, similar to the opening theme of a news program.*)

"Newsflash" (*Skit*)

(*For one female and two male actors*)

Marissa: Good morning, this is Marissa Moretti. We interrupt your regularly scheduled worship service to bring you breaking news from the Galilean hillside. Our reporter, Stanley Prefountaine, has been following this story.

Prefountaine: Marissa, we are here at the base of the mountain. Rumor has it that Jesus and his students Peter, James, and John, have gone up the mountain for a secret meeting. Although extensive questioning was conducted here at base camp, no one seems to have an explanation for this peculiar behavior. Let's check with this person in the crowd. Sir, could I have your name please?

Elias: Elias, Mr. Elias. I'm a local fisherman—Lake Galilee, you know.

Prefountaine: Mr. Elias, what can you tell us about Jesus and what's happening today?

Elias: Well, I don't really know Jesus well. But I will tell you he's a powerful speaker. What he says makes sense for my life. I like to break away from fishing whenever possible to go to one of his lectures. I came today because I needed a breath of fresh air, if you know what I mean.

Prefountaine: What can you tell us, Mr. Elias, about this disappearing act of Jesus with his three students?

Elias: It's not that uncommon. It seems that these guys are the ones closest to Jesus, if you know what I mean. But this meeting is different. Seems they've been up there for some time.

Prefountaine: Do you have any knowledge of the plan for this meeting?

Elias: Me? No, not me. I don't get involved.

Prefountaine: Thank you, Mr. Elias. Wait a minute! There seems to be some action up on the mountain. It appears that Jesus and the students are coming down to join the crowd. I've seen Jesus before, but there seems to be something different about him now. Sorry, folks, the crowds have swirled around Jesus and the students. There doesn't seem to be any way to get to him. The word among the crowd is that Jesus has had a meeting with Moses and Elijah.

Marissa: Stanley, what did people say happened at this meeting?

Prefountaine: Apparently, as Jesus was praying, his face seemed to change and his clothes became dazzling white. The disciples witnessed Moses and Elijah standing with him, having a conversation.

Marissa: How did the disciples respond to this?

Prefountaine: Peter, the lead disciple, is reported to have asked Jesus if they could build three shelters on the mountain: one for each of the leaders—Jesus, Moses, and Elijah. Jesus evidently told him that would not be prudent.

Marissa: Is there any further information?

Prefountaine: Word has it that God spoke to the disciples from a cloud, and told them to be quiet and listen to Jesus. Jesus told them not to spread the word.

Marissa: We'll take care of that.

Prefountaine: Evidently it was quite an interesting spectacle! This is Stanley Prefountaine reporting. Back to you, Marissa.

Marissa: Thank you, Stanley, for that late breaking report. We now return you to your regularly scheduled worship service, already in progress.

Worship Focus: (*Worship Leader*)
From the ordinary reflections of the day,
      the disciples encounter Jesus in a new light,
Transformed before their eyes,
      shining with the brightness of God's Glory.

Songs: "Shine, Jesus, Shine," TFWS, no. 2173 *(See also MGB and WOW Orange.)*
"Open the Eyes of My Heart" by Paul Baloche *(See WOW Blue or iWOR.)*

Prayer Time
Sung Response: "In the Secret" by Andy Park *(Sing refrain twice.)*
(See DMC or WOW Orange.)

Message Movers

Blindness is not limited to lack of eyesight. Our hearts and spirits can be blinded by our own attitudes and preconceptions.

Jesus took Peter, the bold leader among the disciples, and James and John, the volatile "sons of thunder," up on the mountain. There were certain things they would need to know about the authority given to Jesus. They would need to be prepared for the hard journey ahead. In the presence of these disciples, Jesus stands in conversation with Moses, the bringer of the Law, and Elijah, God's major prophet to Israel. Jesus' presence with Moses and Elijah confirms his identity as God's Son. The new covenant will be established.

Peter's immediate reaction is to mark the place where this event occurred. He does not understand what is happening. The voice from the cloud commands the disciples to be silent and to listen to Jesus. They could not stay up on the mountain, in the rarified atmosphere. There was still much work to be done in the valley below.

Song: "The Mountain" by Steven Curtis Chapman *(See* Heaven in the Real World *CD, Steven Curtis Chapman)*

(This may be a presentation piece, or you may play the CD recording.)

We are called to pay attention, to open the eyes of our hearts. Jesus has called us to be in ministry in the valley, strengthened by the witness of his glory and confidence in his love. Jesus has come not as a hero figure, but to demonstrate God's eternal love for us. He offers to us a new model for living together and for caring for the world.

This is a time for active involvement in the reconciliation of the world. Our spiritual eyes must be opened to the vision of service and hope for the world. The trip down the mountain does not lead to our safety; it leads to the cross and beyond.

Offering: "More Like You," TFWS, no. 2167

Opportunities for Service

Closing Song: "Shine, Jesus, Shine," TFWS, no. 2173 *(See also MGB and WOW Orange.)* *(Refrain, Stanza 3, Refrain)*

Sending Forth
Go forth into the world with the assurance of God's glorious presence with you.
Proclaim the wondrous, transforming power of God in your words and in your lives. Go in peace.

(Worship music leaders may play/sing "Shine, Jesus, Shine" as the congregation exits.)

Service 5: "Heart Vision" Visual Resources and Ideas

DESIGN CONCEPT

Three symbolic items are reminders of Moses, Jesus, and Elijah: the burning bush for Moses, the cross for Jesus, and the scroll for Elijah. Represent the three disciples—Peter, James and John—by three green candles. Use white netting to symbolize the cloud out of which the voice of God spoke. The burlap represents the earth. We chose blue for the background, which is not a typical color for the Transfiguration, but we felt that the items stood out well against the blue as opposed to the starkness of the traditional white or off-white.

DESIGN AND DISPLAY SUPPLIES AND RESOURCES

Structure

Use the long riser (66" x 12" x 6") at the back of the table.

Fabric

Cover the table with ten yards of blue cotton, draping the fabric across the back and weaving it across the front. Let it "puddle" on the floor to soften the hard edge of the table. Place ten yards of white netting, doubled, behind the cross, the "burning bush," and the scroll, and drape down the sides of the table. Tuck the netting around the base of the bush to obscure the plastic pot. Drape an eight-yard piece of tightly woven burlap over the center of the back top riser. It comes down the center of the table and is bunched up to create a series of folds. Drop the remainder of the burlap down to the floor and angle toward the left of the table.

Candles

Three green candles represent the disciples: one 10-inch, one 8-inch, and one 6-inch.

Florals and Plants

Place a very large leafy plant in a tall plant stand and put behind the table. Add two spiky plants and a small jade plant on the back, top riser. On the main level of the table, position a small Boston fern. Put two rubber tree plants on the floor in front of the right corner of the table.

Other Items

Place the brass cross on top of the burlap at the center of the back top riser. Create a "burning bush" by taking a plastic plant container, inserting florist foam and sticking in branches clipped from dead trees and bushes. Put stones in the pot to keep it from tipping over. Weave two strips of yellow and red ribbon into the bush to give it the effect of a flame. Use the scroll from Service 1.

SPECIAL NOTES

Floral foam is an inexpensive investment, and it can be used in a variety of settings to secure small florals.

VISUAL RESOURCES

- Fabric: Ten yards of blue cotton, ten yards of white netting, and eight yards of burlap, purchased from local fabric store
- Plants: Most borrowed from Bud's Florist and Greenhouse
- Jade plant: Borrowed from Jerry and Barbara Popp, members of the visual arts team
- Green candles: From Nancy Townley's home
- Brass cross: From the vestibule table of St. Paul's UMC
- Branches, rocks, and plastic plant pot: From Jerry Popp, member of the arts team
- Red and yellow ribbons and floral foam: From Nancy Townley's Holy Hardware supply, woven in the branches by Lesley Leonard, a member of the visual arts team

WORSHIP RESOURCES

"In the Secret," DMC songbook, p. 47 and CD, disc B. See also WOW Orange songbook, p. 103 and CD, orange disc. Solo tracks available from Praise Hymn Soundtracks.

"More Like You," TFWS, no. 2167.

"Open the Eyes of My Heart," WOW Blue songbook, p. 114 and CD, yellow disc. See also iWOR songbook, CD set, DVD "A," and multiformat tracks.

"Shine, Jesus, Shine," TFWS, no. 2173. See also MGB, no. 238; or WOW Orange songbook, p. 133 and CD, cyan disc.

"The Mountain," by Steven Curtis Chapman, *Heaven in the Real World*. Songbook available from Hal Leonard Corporation; CD from The Sparrow Corporation.

ADDITIONAL RESOURCES

"Here I Am to Worship," WA songbook, p. 74 and CD. See also iWOR, DVD "D" and multiformat tracks.

"His Sacred Light," CCJ, no. 15 (suitable for a soloist).

"Into the Image of God," by Howard G. White (Abingdon Press), an upbeat Transfiguration anthem for two-part mixed voices and keyboard.

"Lord, Be Glorified," TFWS, no. 2150.

"Open Our Eyes, Lord," TFWS, no. 2086. See also MGB, no. 59 or WOW Blue songbook, p. 110 and CD, blue disc.

"Open the Eyes of Our Hearts," CC, no. 51.

"Righteous One," MGB, no. 144.

"Swiftly Pass the Clouds of Glory," TFWS, no. 2102 (text only).

"Take My Life," DMC songbook, p. 76 and CD, disc B. See also WOW Blue songbook, p. 131 and CD, blue disc.

"We Have Come at Christ's Own Bidding," TFWS, no. 2103. For information regarding a 1950s doo-wop arrangement of this tune, contact Nylea Butler-Moore at nbmoosic@aol.com.

Heart Vision

Musical Invitation *(Worship Music Leaders)*

"Newsflash" *(Skit)*

Worship Focus

Songs: "Shine, Jesus, Shine" by Graham Kendrick
"Open the Eyes of My Heart" by Paul Baloche

Prayer Time

Sung Response: "In the Secret" by Andy Park *(Sing refrain twice.)*

Message

Song: "The Mountain" by Steven Curtis Chapman

Offering: "More Like You" by Scott Wesley Brown

Opportunities for Service

Closing Song: "Shine, Jesus, Shine" *(Refrain, Stanza 3, Refrain)*

Sending Forth

6. Working with the Clay
(Lent/Ordinary Time)

Musical Invitation: "The Potter's Hand" by Darlene Zschech *(Worship Music Leaders) (Instruments only)*

(See Shout to the Lord 2000, *Lloyd Larson's SATB arrangement, or iWOR.)*

Greeting One Another

(Invite the congregants to greet and welcome one another.)

Songs: "More Love, More Power" by Jude Del Hierro
      "Take My Life" by Scott Underwood

(Both songs are in DMC and WOW Blue. "More Love, More Power" is also in MGB.)

Opportunities for Service

Song: "Change My Heart, O God," TFWS, no. 2152
      (Consider playing in a Latin style.)

(See also DMC, MGB, and WOW Blue.)

Scripture Reading: Jeremiah 18:1-4 *(Worship Leader)*

(While the scripture is being read, use one of the following two options: (1) Keyboardist quietly plays part of "The Potter's Hand" by Darlene Zschech; (2) If you do not have a live potter who will be able to throw the clay later in the service, borrow from the local library a video of a potter throwing clay on a wheel. Show the video during the reading, turning off the soundtrack.)

"Average Joe and Way-Above-Average God" *(Skit)*

(For two actors: "Joe" could be "Jo," and "God" could be either male or female.)

Joe: I never do anything right. Just when I think I've got things in order, they go crazy on me. Ray does everything perfectly—he's got the Midas touch. I've never seen him fail. Some people have all the talents. Me, I'm just an average "Joe"—worker at all trades, master of nothing, not even my own life. Where did I go wrong? God, please help me. I sure would like to do something well.

God: Before anyone else even saw your face, I loved you. I have given you all the special gifts you will ever need. I do not create inferior products. I create wonder and love. Look deep inside. You are incredibly special, unique. I have fashioned you as a witness to the hope for all people.

Joe: But, God, couldn't I just have one special gift?

God: You've already got it—my eternal love. Proclaim that gift in all that you say and do. Live that gift.

Joe: Live the gift of God's love? *(Pause)* Well, I suppose I can do that. I've always been good at helping others discover their unique gifts. Maybe I don't have to be able to do everything perfectly. I'll try to let God take care of that. *(Keyboardist plays softly the introduction of "The Potter's Hand" as Joe delivers the final lines.)* Keep near me, God. Thank you for reminding me of your love for me.
(If you are using a live potter, as soon as the dialogue ends, the potter begins to throw the clay on the wheel. The throwing should continue through the message.)

Song: "The Potter's Hand" by Darlene Zschech

(A soloist sings the stanza, and the other worship music leaders join on the refrain. Soloist sings the stanza again, congregation joins on the refrain.)

Prayer Time

At the beginning of prayer time:
Creative and Healing God, each one of us is uniquely
      designed by you.
Your imprint of love is placed on our hearts.
You know us inside and out and you prize each one
      of us fully.
When we are broken and hurting,
      either by our own devices or by the cruelty of the
      world, you weep for us.
Hear our prayers for each other and for this
      broken and fragile world.
Help us to be witnesses to your steadfast love and
      hope. Amen.

(Pray for one another and then pray for the world's people.)
Sung Response: "The Potter's Hand" by Darlene
      Zschech *(Two refrains)*

Message Movers

The Potter has selected the clay. His tools are his wheel and his hands. He uses water to smooth out the clay and to help shape the vessel. The Potter has a great deal of experience working with the clay. He knows all its properties and its foibles, its texture and temperature. Not everything goes well each time the potter throws the clay. Time after time the vessel fails in his hands. The prophets and the people wonder about the clay and the potter. They voice impatience when they ask, "Why don't you throw out this clay?" This idea has occurred to the Potter, but his loving response is, "You don't waste good clay. You find ways to work with it, to shape it." Again the Potter picks up the clay and continues to smooth it out—again feeling both the texture and the temperature. The Potter is focused on the clay; all the Potter's skill, love, and energy are put into forming this vessel.

"If at first you don't succeed, try, try again," the ancient adage goes. The Potter will continue to work with the clay. The Potter knows the clay, and, trusting in its properties and in the skills he possesses, he fashions a beautiful, durable vessel.

God is fashioning us. Even though we stumble and fall and fail at many things, God is still willing to work with our good "clay." God sees in us that which we cannot see in ourselves—we are of value, we can be vessels for truth, justice, and peace.

Song: "Treasure of You" by Steven Curtis Chapman

(See Heaven in the Real World songbook and CD.)

(This may be a presentation piece, or you may play the CD recording and take the offering at this time. Potter completes the vessel during this song.)

Offering

(If you are using live music, play an instrumental version of "Treasure of You" as the offering is being taken. During the offering, the potter brings the completed vessel forward, placing it on the communion table or in another visible location.)

Song: "He Who Began a Good Work in You," TFWS, no. 2163 *(Sing three times.)*

Sending Forth
God is fashioning us.
   Even though we stumble and fall,
God is still willing to work with us.
   He who began a good work in you will complete it.
Go in peace.
(Worship music leaders may play "He Who Began a Good Work in You" as the congregation exits.)

(If you have a live potter, consider inviting the potter and congregants to create a piece of art after the service is over.

Choose a simple design in advance, such as a cross or other Christian symbol. Place a work table in a location where making a potential mess isn't an issue. Use small slabs of clay to "build" the design, asking participants to add their own unique touches to the slabs. Glaze and fire the clay. Then display the creation in the church as a reminder of the Great Potter's love for us.)

Service 6. "Working with the Clay" Visual Resources and Ideas

DESIGN CONCEPT

Because the traditional color for Lent is purple, you may again use the purple cotton fabric from Services 1 and 2 as the base color. Use approximately fifty feet of landscaping fabric to symbolize the rough earth. Pottery, both whole and broken, and the large jugs and pots symbolize the potter's trade. The candle on the right side of the table represents God's love given to humankind. The candle placed inside the center terra-cotta pot represents the receiving of that light by humankind. The snake, spike, and jade plants are good choices for this "desert" landscape. Angular lines, rather than the soft lines that some leafy plants afford, are desired. Place rocks on the floor in front of the table as symbolic of the rugged landscape and the earthy element of stone.

DESIGN AND DISPLAY SUPPLIES AND RESOURCES

Structure

Use the long table riser (66" x 12" x 6") at the back of the table. Behind the central terra-cotta pot, position a small block to keep it from rolling around. Place a milk crate in front of the table for the broken pottery and stones.

Fabric

Drape ten yards of purple cotton over the back table riser, across the table, and down the front. The fabric should spill down in front of the table onto the main floor of the sanctuary. Drape a fifty-foot piece of landscaper's burlap (the kind used to drape over bushes to protect them from the winter cold) in loops over the back, across the front, and spilling down onto the floor, across the milk crate. Drape some of the burlap around the plant bases. Keep the fabric "puddled" to create a texture for this display.

Candles

Use a six-inch purple pillar candle on the main level of the table. Place a four-inch purple candle in the terra-cotta pot at the center of the table.

Florals and Plants

Choose spiky, angular plants to give drama to the worship setting. Put small spiky plants on the top of the back table riser and surround them with burlap. Place two snake plants near the table, with the jade plant being placed on the floor by the right corner of the table.

Other Items

Several terra-cotta pots and broken pieces add to the scene. Place two broken, terra-cotta plant trays on the main level of the table. Place large earthenware jugs in various areas of the table and a medium-sized two-handled pot on the main level of the table. Position large rocks around the base of the table, one in front of the milk crate, and others near the other large plants. Scatter small groups of stones and pebbles on the table and on the milk crate by the broken terra-cotta pots.

SPECIAL NOTES

Storage is continually a problem for the visual artist. Have a small collection of broken terra-cotta pots for displays, but do not collect too many. Large rocks can be created from insulating foam.

VISUAL RESOURCES

- Fabric: Ten yards of purple cotton purchased at a local fabric store. A fifty-foot roll of landscaper's burlap purchased at a landscaping store
- Purple pillar candles (four-inch and six-inch): Purchased at a local craft store
- Two-handled jug: Purchased at a local craft store
- Large rocks and small stones: Supplied by Jerry Popp, a member of the visual arts team
- Jade plant and two snake plants: Supplied by Barbara Popp, a member of the visual arts team
- Spiky plants: Borrowed from Bud's Florist and Greenhouse

WORSHIP RESOURCES

"Change My Heart, O God," TFWS, no. 2152. See also DMC Songbook, p. 13 and CD, disc B; MGB, no. 16; or WOW Blue Songbook, p. 20 and CD, yellow disc.

"He Who Began a Good Work in You," TFWS, no. 2163. See also OGR, p. 64.

"More Love, More Power," DMC songbook, p. 66 and CD, disc B. See also MGB, no. 136 or WOW Blue songbook, p. 98 and CD, blue disc.

"Take My Life," DMC songbook, p. 76 and CD, disc B. See also WOW Blue songbook, p. 131 and CD, blue disc.

"The Potter's Hand," arranged by Lloyd Larson (Hope Publishing Company), SATB. Multiformat tracks also available from iWOR. See also *Shout to the Lord 2000* songbook and CD (Hosanna! Music); and *Extravagant Worship* CD (Hillsong Music), disc 2.

"Treasure of You," by Steven Curtis Chapman, *Heaven in the Real World* songbook (Hal Leonard Corporation); CD available from The Sparrow Corporation.

ADDITIONAL RESOURCES

"Anointing Fall on Me," CC, no. 57.

"Create in Me a Clean Heart," MGB, no. 100.

"Fingerprints of God," by Steven Curtis Chapman, *Speechless* songbook (Hal Leonard Corporation); CD and solo tracks available from Sparrow Records. Visit www.scchapman.com for more information.

"Hands of the Potter," Caedmon's Call, *Back Home* CD (Essential Records). For more information, visit www.caedmonscall.com.

"In His Time," TFWS, no. 2203. See also MGB, no. 45, or WOW Blue songbook, p. 60 and CD, yellow disc.

"Open Our Eyes, Lord," TFWS, no. 2086. See also MGB, no. 59, or WOW Blue songbook, p. 110 and CD, blue disc.

"Praise You," TFWS, no. 2003 (see especially verse 2).

"Refiner's Fire," DMC songbook, p. 69 and CD, disc A, or WOW Blue songbook, p. 121 and CD, yellow disc.

"The Power of Your Love," MGB, no. 157.

"Take My Hand," CC, no. 11.

Working with the Clay

Musical Invitation: "The Potter's Hand" by Darlene Zschech
(Worship Music Leaders)

Greeting One Another

Songs: "More Love, More Power" by Jude Del Hierro
"Take My Life" by Scott Underwood

Opportunities for Service

Song: "Change My Heart, O God" by Eddie Espinosa

Scripture Reading: Jeremiah 18:1-4

"Average Joe and Way-Above-Average God" *(Skit)*

Song: "The Potter's Hand" by Darlene Zschech

Prayer Time
Sung Response: "The Potter's Hand" by Darlene Zschech *(two refrains)*

Message

Song: "Treasure of You" by Steven Curtis Chapman *(Worship Music Leaders or CD)*

Offering

Song: "He Who Began a Good Work in You" by Jon Mohr

Sending Forth

7. Be Healed: Power for the Powerless

(Lent/Ordinary Time/Healing Service)

Musical Invitation *(Worship music leaders may play/sing any of the songs listed below, or an appropriate selection of their choosing.)*

Greeting and Opportunities for Service

Song: "My Life Is in You, Lord," TFWS, no. 2032 *(See also WOW Blue.)*

Worship Focus

L: We come to this place of worship to praise God with all of our strength, our lives, our hopes and our fears.

P: We come here asking God for help and for healing.

L: God hears your cries and offers healing love.

P: We truly want to be healed and restored to God's love.

L: Get ready, for God's healing hand is upon your life.

P: We are ready. Amen.

Songs: "Good to Me" by Craig Musseau *(See DMC and WOW Green.)*
"Out of the Depths," TFWS, no. 2136

Message Movers—Part 1

Jesus is preaching at the home of Simon Peter. Four people arrive carrying a litter upon which lies a paralyzed friend. Seeking healing and restoration for their friend, they try to approach Jesus, but the crowd is too large. They scale a wall and lower the man on the litter through the portico roof. Simon Peter is concerned with the destruction of his property. He will find a new concern in a few minutes.

The man on the litter states that he has been suffering for many years because of his sins and the sins of his parents. Jesus kneels beside him and tells him that his sins are forgiven. Some in the crowd are concerned that Jesus has committed blasphemy. Only God can forgive sins. Jesus asks, "Which is easier, to say 'Your sins are forgiven,' or to say, 'Take up your mat and go home?'" So they may understand the power of God's forgiving love, the man is healed.

The man hesitantly and awkwardly stands up, rejoicing at his newfound mobility. This is a scene of hope and triumph, as well as amazement and consternation.

Video Clip: Jesus heals the paralytic (from *Jesus of Nazareth*)
VHS, Tape 2: START—12:56. Simon Peter says, "Wait, what are you doing to my property?"
STOP—15:31. Screen goes to black.

Looking at this scene, we might determine that the paralyzed man wanted to be healed, but perhaps wondered if this was even remotely possible since he had been a paralytic for so many years. Perhaps we would have the same doubts and fears. We want to be healed, we think; but we have lived in the paralyzed state for so long that it has become familiar. If we are healed, what will life be like for us? Will we know how to function? Will we have newfound responsibilities? For some, it is easier to live in the paralytic state than to risk healing.

Healing is not the same thing as being cured. We may be healed of our affliction, but the fear of the disease's possible return can remain with us. True healing occurs when we let go of the affliction and its control over us.

(If someone in your congregation has experienced healing, ask him or her to give a testimony here. The following is an example.)

Lesley, a member of St. Paul's UMC in Castleton, New York, had stage-4 lung cancer. Her summer months were spent in great pain as a result of chemotherapy. In the midst of the bone pain, the numbness in hands and feet, and the scorching heat of the summer months, Lesley wondered whether or not she would make it through each day; but she persisted in her belief that healing was possible. On March 7, 2003, Lesley received the news from the oncologist that there was little evidence of the cancer, which once threatened to claim her life. Had the chemotherapy healed her, or the four-month-long drug program of Iressa? Or had something else worked within her to offer her strength for healing?

Song: "I Can Hear Your Voice" by Michael W. Smith, Debbie Smith, and Whitney Smith
(*Worship music leaders, featuring a soloist*)

Message Movers—Part 2

Do we want to be healed? Healing takes great inner strength and courage. It asks us to "walk by faith and not by sight." Lesley (*or the person who gave a testimony earlier*) placed her whole trust in God.

(*If you used a testimony, tailor the following to fit that person's experience.*)

Long before the cancer was discovered, Lesley felt called by God to become a minister. The illness threatened that direction for her life, but her faith in God's call was strong. Her doctors credit her inner strength and determination with being critical components in her present situation. She still wonders what each day will bring, but she commits each moment to God's care for whatever time or opportunities she may have to serve. Lesley says that one of the major components in her healing is the community of faith. The community offered prayers, support, and love to her throughout her ordeal. It celebrated each little bit of good news and placed its trust in God's healing power and love.

Healing is not just about curing an illness. Too often our lives are broken, hurt, bruised. We have been torn apart by broken relationships and events that make us feel unworthy and of little value. Brokenness exists on many levels of spiritual living. Where do we find brokenness, infection, and bruising in our lives? Jesus calls to us, "Do not be afraid, I am with you. I have called you each by name." Do we dare trust Jesus to heal us? We are powerless to provide our own healing, no matter how many self-help books we read or how many crystals we rub. Our healing comes from the encounter with Jesus, who asks us if we really want to be healed.

Song: "You Are Mine," TFWS, no. 2218

Prayer Time
(*Read individual stanzas of Fred Pratt Green's hymn text, "O Christ, the Healer," UMH, no. 265, or another poem/hymn text that focuses on healing, with directed prayers for healing between each stanza.*)

Read stanza 1 and 2 of the chosen hymn/poem.
(*Insert prayers of healing for individuals here.*)

Read stanza 3 of the chosen hymn/poem.
(*Insert prayers for ourselves, for healing and forgiveness here.*)

Read stanza 4 of the chosen hymn/poem.
(*Insert prayers of healing for a broken world.*)

Read stanza 5 of the chosen hymn/poem.
(*Close with "Amen."*)

Optional Healing Service
(*Provide three "prayer stations" staffed with worship leaders or members of your prayer ministry. These prayer leaders will lay hands on and pray with those persons who desire healing. While soothing instrumental music is being played, invite congregants to come to a prayer station, if they wish. As the people come forward, the Worship Leader reads James 5:14-15. Music and prayer suggestions are listed in Additional Resources below.*)

Message Movers—Part 3
God said to us, "Rise up, be healed, take your mat, and walk!"
And now we are standing, walking, running, dancing, leaping.
God took care of us when we were helpless and powerless.
Now it is our turn to help others—we have experienced the healing!
Are we willing to be ambassadors for Christ?
If so, we must go where others are in need of healing.
We don't wait for those in need to come to us.

Segue into the Offering (*Worship Leader*)
As Christ has healed us, we are called to be a healing presence for others. We are invited to support the healing ministries of the church. Let us then receive, with great joy, our morning offering.

Offering:/Closing Song: "Oh, I Know the Lord's Laid His Hands on Me," TFWS, 2139
(*The worship music leaders, or choir, sings the song during the offering. When the offering is collected, the congregation is invited to stand and join in the singing.*)

Sending Forth
We know that our sins are forgiven.
    We are cleansed of our pain.
Jesus has washed away all our sins.
    as Christ stretched out his hand for our healing,
May we be a healing presence for Christ in this broken and hurting world. Amen.

Sending Forth Song: "May You Run and Not Be Weary," TFWS, no. 2281
(*See also CC songbook and CD.*)

(*Worship music leaders may play/sing "May You Run and Not Be Weary" or a selection of their choice as the congregation exits.*)

Service 7. "Be Healed: Power for the Powerless" Visual Resources and Ideas

DESIGN CONCEPT

Flowing water is often associated with healing. Use a supple blue fabric to represent water. Create the sense of water cascading down from a working fountain at the top of the display and falling into a gentle pool at the base of the display. This is a serene setting.

DESIGN AND DISPLAY SUPPLIES AND RESOURCES

Structure

Use the long table riser at the back of the table, a two-inch block on the top of the riser for the candle, and a six-inch-square riser for the Boston fern at the top of the back table riser. Add a milk crate down in front of the table to give an additional sense of "spill."

Fabric

The ten yards of purple cotton that was purchased for the Advent table, is used as a base for this display. Beginning at the top back riser, "spill" the fifty feet of landscaper's burlap (which represents the ground) down over the left corner of the table, and the rest down the middle of the table. "Puddle" the remaining burlap on the floor, around the base of some of the plants. Use eight yards of blue silkene for the "water." It drapes well and simulates water as it flows downward.

Candles

Only one 6-inch purple pillar candle is used. Place it on the top of the back table riser.

Florals and Plants

Don't be afraid to go "all out" for plants in this lush setting. Place a large Boston fern on the riser at the back of the table. Drape artificial ivy down from the candle to the main table level. To the left of the blue "waterfall," place two small Boston ferns. On the right of the "flowing water" on the main table level, place two spiky plants. Position one large potted palm on a medium-sized plant stand on the left side of the table. Place another large potted palm on the floor in front of the other palm. Put the small snake plant at the left corner of the table, and set the large jade plant and the rubber tree plant on the immediate left of the "waterfall" near the base of the table. On the right side of the table, on the floor, arrange the large leafy plant and the large snake plant.

Other Items

Place a working fountain (we used terra-cotta) on the upper left of the back table riser, on the blue fabric. Put large rocks on the floor in front of the table and arrange them around the "blue pool." Scatter white marble chips around the pool and the rocks on the floor and also near the edge of the blue fabric on the main table level.

SPECIAL NOTES

Silkene is a wonderful lining fabric, but it should be treated carefully. It will ravel.

VISUAL RESOURCES

- Fabric: Ten yards of purple cotton and eight yards of blue silkene, purchased at a local fabric store; burlap purchased at a landscaping store
- Fountain: Owned by Nancy Townley
- Candle: Purchased from local craft store
- Large plants: Borrowed from Bud's Florist and Greenhouse
- Rocks and marble chips, snake and jade plants: Borrowed from Jerry and Barbara Popp, members of the visual arts team

WORSHIP RESOURCES

"Good to Me," DMC songbook, p. 32 and CD, disc A. See also WOW Green songbook, p. 54 and CD, disc 2.

"I Can Hear Your Voice," WA songbook, p. 41 and CD.

Jesus of Nazareth video (Artisan); available in VHS or DVD format.

"May You Run and Not Be Weary," TFWS, no. 2281. See also or CC, no. 73 and CD.

"My Life Is in You Lord," TFWS, no. 2032. See also WOW Blue songbook, p. 106 and CD, blue disc. Solo tracks also available from Daywind Music Group.

"O Christ, the Healer," UMH, no. 265 (text only).

"Oh, I Know the Lord's Laid His Hands on Me," TFWS, no. 2139. Anthem arrangement by Alice Parker, "I Know the Lord" (GIA Publications, Inc.), SATB, a cappella with medium-voice solo. Recorded by Alice Parker, Pamela Warrick-Smith, and Melodious Accord on Take Me to the Water; available in CD or cassette format.

"Out of the Depths," TFWS, no. 2136.

"You Are Mine," TFWS, no. 2218. Recorded by David Haas on You Are Mine; available in CD or cassette format from GIA Publications, Inc.

ADDITIONAL RESOURCES

"Come Just As You Are," MGB, no. 179. See also WOW Green songbook, p. 26 and CD, disc 2. Solo tracks available from Praise Hymn Soundtracks.

"Draw Me into Your Presence," MGB, no. 23.

"Give Thanks," TFWS, no. 2036. See also OGR, p. 52.

"Heal Me, Hands of Jesus," UMH, no. 262.

"Heal Us, Emmanuel," a two-part, original composition in a pop ballad style by Nylea Butler-Moore, featuring strains of "There Is a Balm in Gilead." For information, contact Nylea at nbmoosic@aol.com.

"I Will Cast All My Cares," CC, no. 39.

"Let Your Soul Be Your Pilot," recorded by Sting on *Mercury Falling* (A & M Records, Inc.).

"Lord, Be Glorified," TFWS, no. 2150.

"Lord, Listen to Your Children," TFWS, no. 2207.

"My Peace," MGB, no. 53.

Prayers in UMH: "For the Sick," no. 457; "The Serenity Prayer," no. 459; "In Time of Illness," no. 460; "An Invitation to Christ," no. 466; "For God's Gifts," no. 489.

"Trading My Sorrows," WOW Green songbook, p. 155 and CD, disc 1. See also iWOR (songbook, CD set, DVD "B," and multiformat trax).

With Hope and Healing, a CD by Stephen Petrunak featuring soothing instrumental music influenced by health, hope, and the healing process. Available in CD or cassette format from GIA Publications, Inc.

Be Healed: Power for the Powerless

Musical Invitation (*Worship Music Leaders*)

Greeting and Opportunities for Service

Song: "My Life Is In You, Lord" by Daniel Gardner

Worship Focus
L: We come to this place of worship to praise God
   with all of our strength, our lives, our hopes and our fears.
P: We come here asking God for help and for healing.
L: God hears your cries and offers healing love.
P: We truly want to be healed and restored to God's love.
L: Get ready, for God's healing hand is upon your life.
P: We are ready. Amen.

Songs: "Good to Me" by Craig Musseau
   "Out of the Depths" by Ruth Duck and Robert J. Batastini

Message—Part 1
Video Clip: Jesus heals the paralytic (*From* Jesus of Nazareth)

Song: "I Can Hear Your Voice" by Michael W. Smith, Debbie Smith, and
   Whitney Smith (*Worship Music Leaders*)

Message—Part 2

Song: "You Are Mine" by David Haas

Prayer Time

Optional Healing Service

Message, Part 3

Offering/Closing Song: "Oh, I Know the Lord's Laid His Hands on Me"
   (*traditional spiritual*)

Sending Forth

Sending Forth Song: "May You Run and Not Be Weary" by Paul Murakami and
   Handt Hanson

God calls us to identify with the poor

8. Open Hands
(Lent)

Musical Invitation (*Worship music leaders may play/sing any of the songs listed below, or an appropriate selection of their choosing.*)

"Ethel and the Girls" (*Skit*)
(*Four or five ladies, well dressed, are seated in a semicircle. One of the ladies, Ethel, wearing a flowered hat and holding a pair of white gloves, is speaking to the other women, who seem to hang on her every word.*)

Ethel: Ladies, ladies, I am so delighted that you have agreed to be our Sunday morning Greeters. As you know, this is a prestigious position. You are on the front lines of the church. You will make the most important and lasting impression. Pastor is relying on us to show how wonderful we (that is, our church) are. Now here are some important things to remember:

Always wear lovely print or flowered dresses, making sure that your shoes and your hat match or are complementary. Never wear a pantsuit. Women should not wear slacks in church—it's just too casual and manly. We want to offer our best to the Lord, don't we?

Observe these gloves, if you will. I have taken the liberty of purchasing gloves for each greeter. You must under all circumstances wear the gloves when greeting people. You never know where people have been—dirty hands, diseases; you know what I mean. Gloves must be laundered and bleached every week—there will be no grimy or dull gloves at our doors!

Never shake hands fully gripping the hand of the person. Extend only your fingers and give a very light handshake. You are not pumping a well handle! A little shake is sufficient, and then politely remove your hand. Turn the person over to the ushers, who will lead them in the sanctuary. The ushers know what they are supposed to do and where to seat the people. Also never shake hands or speak with children—your business is to greet the adults.

Last, but certainly not least, watch for the people who are well dressed and obviously in the more desirable class of society. We need people of status in our church—we are on the cutting edge, if you will forgive the vernacular, of mission and we want only the best people here. After all, they will have the best ideas, know-how, and funding resources to do whatever we want.

Ladies, please remember that we are the church of "Open Hearts, Open Minds, Open Doors."

Thank you for coming. You are dismissed—oh, don't forget your gloves!

Worship Focus (*Worship Leader*)
Believe it or not, "Ethel and the Girls" was inspired by real events.
The crux of the story is this—
    we want to present our best selves to others and to God, but we sometimes do this at the expense of the mission to which Christ calls us.
We are more concerned about appearance and propriety than we are about persons.
What is truly our best offering for the Lord?
What is the cry of our hearts?

Songs: "Cry of My Heart," TFWS, no. 2165 (*See also DMC and WOW Green.*)
    "Open Our Hearts" by Nylea L. Butler-Moore
(*See Worship Resources for ordering information.*)

Message Movers
We are deluged from all sides by requests for assistance. Every time we turn around, there is a financial campaign for some cause or another, pleading for our financial assistance. Often our response is to turn a deaf ear, to discard the letter for financial help, to turn our back on poverty. It is sometimes too much for us to bear—we cannot solve all the problems of the world, so we choose not to solve any of them.

Our monetary gifts help, but more important is the commitment of our time and spirit, which will win the battle. Our compassion is critical and cannot be measured solely in dollars and cents. It is measured in our time and witness to Christ's claim on our lives.

The local food pantries were conducting their Thanksgiving request for canned and boxed foods to stock their shelves for people in need. The response was poor. At the same time the news media reported that a particular brand of cranberries might be contaminated. Suddenly the food pantry began to receive large quantities of canned goods, most of which were the cranberries mentioned in the report. This may not seem like such a dilemma to some people, but none of us would want to risk eating food that might be contaminated. Yet, there they were, hundreds of cans of cranberries.

Do we give only of our leftovers or do we commit the very best we have in service to others? Imagine, for a moment, what it would be like to be in need of food. You don't have enough money to adequately feed your family, but you earn too much to qualify for food stamps. As difficult as it is, you go to the local food pantry, and the people are delighted to serve you. They are kind and want to help in any way they can. When you get home, you notice that almost all of the canned goods, donated lovingly to the food pantry by local people, are dented and some are even rusted. How do you feel?

Some people say, "Beggars can't be choosers." How would we feel saying that to Christ if he asked us how we helped others? "Beggars can't be choosers"—that telling phrase says more than we care to admit.

Jesus challenged his disciples to think beyond their own "comfort zones." *(If you want to read Matthew 25:35-40, insert it here.)* He said that he was ill-clothed, hungry, thirsty, lost, alone, sick, imprisoned, a stranger, and that the disciples offered clothing, food and beverage, companionship and welcome to him. They wanted to know when he experienced all those things and when they helped to meet his needs. He stated that when they did these things for anyone, they did them for him.

When we give our dented and rusting cans, our torn and soiled clothing, a limp handshake, an insincere smile, or a cursory welcome, we should ask ourselves if we would give these same things to Christ. When we turn our backs on opportunities to help others, or even to support those who do such work, we turn our backs on Christ.

If we are to follow Christ fully, we must give fully. We must open our hands in service, compassion, and hope for others. *(If yours is not a UMC church, delete the next phrase.)*

We, in The United Methodist Church, claim to be the church of "Open Hearts, Open Minds, and Open Doors." If this is the case, then we can give no less than our best in reaching out to others—in doing so, we will have ministered to Christ.

Song: "Screen Door" by Rich Mullins *(See Rich Mullins's* Songs *CD and songbook.)*
(This may be a presentation piece, or you may play the CD recording while showing a collection of photographs of people in need.)

Responsive Reading
L1: Open your hearts and your spirits as you hear the voice of God speaking to you,
  inviting you to come.
L2: "Come to me, dear one. Open your hands."
P: I can't, Lord. My hands are dirty.

L1: "Open your hands and I will offer you cleansing water and soft towels."
L2: "Come to me, dear friend. Open your hands."
P: I can't, Lord. My hands are bloody and scarred.
L1: "Open your hands and I will give you healing balm."
L2: "Come to me, blessed child. Open your hands."
P: I can't, Lord. I'm not important. I have nothing to give.
L1/L2: "Open your hands and receive my gentle hand of blessing."

Quiet Moments in Prayer
(Each petition is followed by silence.)

Let us pray for those who are ill and who mourn . . . *(silence)*
Let us pray for all people who are lonely, lost, and alienated . . . *(silence)*
Let us pray for this broken and hurting world . . . *(silence)*
Let us pray for ourselves that we may be faithful to you, O God . . . *(silence)*

Sung Response: "Lord God, Almighty," TFWS, no. 2006 *(Stanza 1 only)*
(Consider using guitar accompaniment only—keep it simple.)

Opportunities for Service

"Open Your Hand": Deuteronomy 15:10-11 *(Worship Leader reads scripture.)*

Offering/Song: "I'm Gonna Live So God Can Use Me," TFWS, no. 2153
(If possible, have a soloist sing stanza 1 in a slow tempo, engaging in musical dialogue with a lead guitarist or keyboardist. Congregation repeats stanza 1 and sings the following stanzas in a boogie-woogie style, upbeat tempo.)

Prayer
O Lord, remind us again that you always give us your best, never your leftovers.
Can we do less for you?
  As we serve others, we are serving you.
As we love others, we are loving you.
  Help us remember that always. Amen.

Sending Forth Song: "Sent Out in Jesus' Name," TFWS, no. 2184
(The worship music leaders may sing the song one complete time in Spanish and then invite the congregation to sing the song in English.)
(Worship music leaders may play "Sent Out in Jesus' Name" as the congregation exits.)

Service 8. "Open Hands"
Visual Resources and Ideas

DESIGN CONCEPT

One of the themes of The United Methodist Church is the church of "Open Hearts, Open Minds, and Open Doors." Our visual design team suggested that "Open Hands" should be added to this. The table drape represents the hands of people reaching out to assist others. The candles are in abundance, as is the spark of God's love in each person. Inadvertently, we discovered that the center spot of most of the hands contains a heart shape. We liked the idea that we put our hearts and our energy into serving others.

DESIGN AND DISPLAY SUPPLIES AND RESOURCES

Structure

Use the back table riser, as well as a music stand behind the table to give additional height for the "hand" drape. Place a milk crate at the base for an additional level.

Fabric

Cover the back tabletop riser and the table with ten yards of purple cotton. "Puddle" the fabric down in front of the table to soften the line. Create the "hand drape" (approximately six feet long and thirty inches wide) using room darkening fabric (canvas drapery liner). Wear rubber gloves and cover hands with acrylic paints. Then place hands on the canvas to create the hand images (acrylics dry rapidly, a distinct advantage).

Candles

Use six 6-inch, two 10-inch, and two 4-inch purple pillar candles.

Florals and Plants

Place potted palms on the right and left of the table, each on medium-sized plant stands. Put the jade plant on the left side of the table. Place a rubber tree plant on the right side of the table. Spiky plants on either side of the "hand drape" give a special accent to the table.

Other Items

Use large stones at the base of the table to give special texture to the design.

SPECIAL NOTES

Room darkening fabric takes acrylic paints well. When it is dry, the art piece can be stored rolled up and placed in a tube, or it can be folded and laid flat.

VISUAL RESOURCES

- Fabric: Ten yards purple cotton, purchased at a local fabric store
- Room darkening fabric: Purchased at a home decorating center
- Candles: Purchased at a local craft store
- Rocks and jade plant: Borrowed from Jerry and Barbara Popp, members of the visual arts team
- Other plants: Borrowed from Bud's Florist and Greenhouse

WORSHIP RESOURCES

"Cry of My Heart," TFWS, no. 2165. See also DMC songbook, p. 20 and CD, disc B or WOW Green songbook, p. 32 and CD, disc 2.

"I'm Gonna Live So God Can Use Me," TFWS, no. 2153.

"Lord God, Almighty," TFWS, no. 2006.

"Open Our Hearts" by Nylea Butler-Moore. Suitable for soloist, worship music leaders, and congregation. For information, contact the composer at nbmoosic@aol.com.

"Screen Door," by Rich Mullins, *Songs* CD (Reunion Records); songbook available from Hal Leonard Corporation.

"Sent Out in Jesus' Name," TFWS, no. 2184.

ADDITIONAL RESOURCES

"Hands and Feet," sung by Audio Adrenaline on *WOW 2001, The Year's 30 Top Christian Artists and Songs* CD, blue disc (EMI Christian Music Group).

"Lord, I Want to Be a Christian," UMH, no. 402. Consider transposing key to D major to make it easier to play on guitar. Works well with guitar and flute. For lead sheet information, contact nbmoosic@aol.com.

"Love Is the Answer," by Todd Rundgren, *Very Best of Todd Rundgren* CD (Rhino Entertainment Company).

"Prayer for the City," MGB, no. 142.

Prayers from UMH: "For Courage to Do Justice," no. 456; "The Prayer of St. Francis," no. 481.

"Say the Words (Now)," DC Talk, *Intermission: The Greatest Hits* CD (ForeFront Records). For a high-energy song with rap sections, consider "Luv Is a Verb" from the same collection.

"Send Me," MGB, no. 237.

"Together We Serve," TFWS, no. 2175.

"What If She's an Angel?" by Tommy Shane Steiner, *Then Came the Night* CD (RCA).

Open Hands

Musical Invitation *(Worship Music Leaders)*

"Ethel and the Girls" *(Skit)*

Worship Focus

Songs: "Cry of My Heart" by Terry Butler
"Open Our Hearts" by Nylea L. Butler-Moore

Message

Song: "Screen Door" by Rich Mullins *(Worship Music Leaders)*

Responsive Reading

L1: Open your hearts and your spirits as you hear the voice of God speaking to you, inviting you to come.

L2: "Come to me, dear one. Open your hands."

P: I can't, Lord. My hands are dirty.

L1: "Open your hands and I will offer you cleansing water and soft towels."

L2: "Come to me, dear friend. Open your hands."

P: I can't, Lord. My hands are bloody and scarred.

L1: "Open your hands and I will give you healing balm."

L2: "Come to me, blessed child. Open your hands."

P: I can't, Lord. I'm not important. I have nothing to give.

L1/L2: "Open your hands and receive my gentle hand of blessing."

Quiet Moments in Prayer
   Sung Response: "Lord God, Almighty" by Coni Huisman *(Stanza 1 only)*

Opportunities for Service

"Open Your Hand": Deuteronomy 15:10-11

Offering/Song: "I'm Gonna Live So God Can Use Me" *(Traditional spiritual)*

Prayer

Sending Forth Song: "Sent Out in Jesus' Name" *(Traditional Cuban)*

9. Kicking the Habit
(Lent)

Musical Invitation (*Worship music leaders may sing/play any of the songs listed below, or an appropriate selection of their choosing.*)

Songs: "Lord, Reign in Me" by Brenton Brown (*See DMC and WOW Green.*)
"Your Name Is Holy" by Brian Doerksen (*See DMC.*)

Greeting and Opportunities for Service

Song: "Lead Me, Guide Me," TFWS, no. 2214
(*Play in a swung, gospel style—treating dotted eighths and sixteenths as triplets. Works well with piano alone, piano and a "Hammond" organ sound, or with band.*)

Video Clip from *The Lion, the Witch, and the Wardrobe*
VHS: START—37:16. Inside pavilion; Witch says, "Now Son of Adam, I'm eager to know all about you."
STOP—41:36. Witch says, "Just think how good it will taste then."
(*Ends with close-up on Edmund.*)

In episode 1 of the BBC's *The Lion, the Witch, and the Wardrobe*, Edmund finds himself in the magical land of Narnia, where he meets the evil White Witch. The Witch, having ulterior motives, asks Edmund what his favorite treat is. Edmund quickly replies "Turkish Delight" candy. In order to entice Edmund to do what she desires, she gives him some enchanted Turkish Delight. Edmund gorges himself on the candy and craves more and more. The desire for the candy becomes a controlling force in his life, and his motives turn evil.

Segue into Prayer Time: In *The Lion, The Witch, and the Wardrobe*, Edmund succumbs to the temptations of Turkish Delight, and he becomes a vicious, greedy person. When we give ourselves to temptations, many things can happen that we did not plan.

Prayer Time
It even surprises us, Generous God,
how greedy we can become.
Temptations are placed before us, and we make a host of excuses for indulging in them rather than showing responsible behavior.
We kid ourselves into excusing our behavior with false promises of repentance or resolutions to do "better" soon.
Help us to be more honest with ourselves and with you.
Make us stand strong when we are tempted by momentary pleasures and satisfactions.
Give us courage to say "No" to those things that are harmful to us and to others.

(*Insert other prayers here as desired.*)

Song: "Lord, Have Mercy" by Steve Merkel (*See WA songbook and CD.*)

(*As the prayer time is drawing to a close, the keyboardist should begin playing the introduction of "Lord, Have Mercy." Ask the person leading the prayers for a cue. A soloist will sing the verses and the worship music leaders will sing the first refrain. Invite the congregation to sing the following refrains. If possible, use a violin or oboe for the solo instrumental part; or play the part on a MIDI keyboard patch and play the accompaniment on piano.*)

Scripture Reading: Matthew 4:1-11

(*As the scripture is read, show the following four slides or graphics.*)
• Verse 3: Loaves of bread and stones
• Verse 5: The pinnacle or spire of a large temple or cathedral
• Verse 8: A night scene of a big city, such as Las Vegas
• Verse 11: A storm darkened sky with rays of light bursting through

(*Use an Internet search engine to find these images online.*)

Song: "Walkin' Through the Wilderness" by Nylea L. Butler-Moore

(*This jazzy song is for Leader and All; the All part could be sung by a small vocal ensemble or the congregation. If someone in your congregation is a tap dancer, consider asking this person to create a tap routine for this song.*)

"Phone Call from Boss Diablo" (*Skit*)
(*For one male actor, dressed in a Mafia-type dark business suit, with several gold rings on his fingers.*)

Boss Diablo: (*On cell phone*) What do you mean, you can't get the people to do what you want? Bribe them! Threaten them! Get rid of them! They don't mean a thing to us. They only help us achieve our goals. When that's done, we can eliminate them. I don't care if they have families or problems. I have a business to run, and if you're too sensitive to take care of this matter, I will definitely find someone else. Okay, I suppose I could give you one more chance. That's part of my charm, my compassion, and my flexibility. But this is it: one more screw up and you're done! Get it? (*Hangs up cell phone and looks up, as though he's talking to God.*)

Lord, it's hard to get good help these days. They are so sensitive, so patient. Not like in the good old days when you could count on greed, malice, avarice, and anger—all the attributes of an especially good employee. Now they worry about every little detail. How do they think they will get to the top in this business by being nice? Nice? Where does that get you? Don't they remember that "Nice guys finish last"?

They have got to think about themselves, not others. "Do what's best for you"—that's the way to live. Take care of number one. What's that old biblical maxim? "Do unto others *before* they do unto you," or something like that. Well, I am not going to let the little wimps get me down.

There was only one who really gave me trouble. Remember him? Alone in the desert, I think. I offered him all the kingdoms of the world—a darn good deal if you ask me! But he wasn't interested. I told him that he could have all the wealth and power anyone could ever want—he didn't want it. If money and power don't work, try threats. "Throw yourself off the top of the building—supposedly God's angels will take care of you." He didn't fall for that either. Even though he was really hungry, he didn't even want to make bread out of stones. Now, that temptation was a no-brainer—everyone falls for that one! Who goes hungry when they don't have to? But, he was different. So, I left him alone for a time.

Then he got people thinking that they could change; that it was critical to help others; to provide assistance for the needy in the world; to not be so grasping; to appreciate everything. He was undermining my work! I try to give the people a steady diet of hate, anger, and bitterness, and he comes along with a diet of compassion, hope, and peace. Hah! A healthy diet, who needs it? We all like to chew the fat, don't we? And what about those decadent little goodies that melt in our mouths? Devils food cupcakes being my personal favorites! Speaking of which— (*Takes out a cupcake and greedily gulps a bite.*) Well, back to work—what shall I put on the menu today?

Message Movers

A significant percentage of Americans are overweight—so say the medical journals. Food is a national obsession. There is even a food channel on TV featuring such notables as Emeril La Gasse, Martha Stewart, the 30-Minute Gourmet, and Sara's Secrets. (*If there are other cooking experts that are more well known in your area, insert their names in place of the above.*) Magazines abound with food ads. Our grocery stores are no longer stores but "supermarkets," with the emphasis on "super." All manner of food stuffs are presented to us for our delight. One of our weaknesses is dessert. Many of us love the sweet stuff, but too much is not good for our health. Some of us even become diabetic from overeating and lack of exercise. Such is the price of self-indulgence.

Lent is often thought of as a time to "give up something" as we prepare for Easter. How many of us have quietly abstained from lima beans and Brussels sprouts during Lent? This is easy because we don't like them to begin with. Some of us consider giving up candy or other junk foods for Lent, but this is often harder than giving up the dreaded green veggies because we like our junk food.

In addition to junk food in our diets, there is "junk food of the mind," which prohibits good, healthy living. Attitudes and actions poison and destroy: gossip, rumor mongering, prejudice, intolerance, bigotry, attitudes of superiority. You know the list. We all have such a list, whether we want to admit it or not. Maybe it's time for a special Lenten "fast," one that releases us from "junk" habits. What about fasting from judging others, from complaining, from worrying, from excluding others because of perceived differences? Can we take a break from pessimism and fatalism? Can we let go of anger, bitterness, alienation, and self-pity? Now that's an interesting fast!

When we kick the habits that have become "junk food" in our lives, a special feast awaits us. When we let go of our pessimism, we begin to believe in the possibilities. When we release our bitterness, we may find room for forgiveness and reconciliation.

We are called during Lent to examine ways in which we have distanced ourselves from Christ and from one another. Experts say that it takes approximately twenty days to establish a habit, good or bad. We have forty days of Lent in which to "Kick the Bad Habit" and "Establish a Good Habit." We are challenged to look at the unity and oneness found in Christ, and to turn away from the things that destroy and divide.

The fast, letting go of harmful ways, will become

a feast of hope and love in Christ Jesus. Herein lies strength, power, and faith. And living in the light of Christ's power is healthful living at its finest!

Song: "In the Light" by Charlie Peacock *(See DC Talk, Intermission: The Greatest Hits CD.)*

(This may be a presentation piece, or you may play the CD recording. If using the CD, present "Hungry" immediately following the message and play the CD recording of "In the Light" during the offering.)

Segue into Offering
You are invited to come forward to renew your
    commitment to the Lord.
You may place your monetary gifts in the baskets
    provided in front.
Receive the gift of a stone, that Jesus refused to turn
    into bread to satisfy his hunger.
Be reminded of the strength that God gives you to
    withstand temptations.

Offering: "Hungry" by Kathryn Scott *(See DMC, WOW Orange, or iWOR.)*

Sending Forth
    May the grace of God, which sustains and satisfies us, keep you always in the Light. Go in peace. Amen.

(Worship music leaders may play "Hungry," "In the Light," or another appropriate selection as the congregation exits.)

Service 9. "Kicking the Habit" Visual Resources and Ideas

DESIGN CONCEPT
    This was one of the harder designs to create. We began to think about the junk food that we consume and wondered if we should put a whole lot of junk food containers on the worship center. We decided against that and began to talk about focusing our lives on God's will for us that will lead to hope and peace. One of the visual art team members suggested a grouping of candles. We tried placing a mirror behind the candle grouping to reflect the candlelight, but because the church's domed ceiling is white, it did not reflect the candlelight, but looked like a large white rectangle. We decided that we liked the cross centered on the table, just as the Christ is central in our lives and that the lighted candles represent the inspiration and healing that we draw from Christ.

DESIGN AND DISPLAY SUPPLIES AND RESOURCES

Structure
    Use the back tabletop riser. Place a milk crate down in front to provide a special level for the large fern.

Fabric
    The purple Lenten fabric remains on the table. No other fabric is used.

Candles
    Group two 10-inch and five 6-inch purple pillar candles, and three 4-inch purple candles on the table surrounding the brass cross.

Florals and Plants
    Place two large Boston ferns as follows: one on the back table top riser and one on the milk crate in front of the table. The spiky plants appear on the floor on either side of the large fern. To the right of the spiky plant is a rubber tree plant. To the left of the other spiky plant is the jade plant. Position the two potted palm plants on medium-sized plant stands on either side of the table.

Other Items
    Put the brass cross on the center of the table in front of the large Boston fern. Scatter rocks on the floor near the floor plants.

SPECIAL NOTES
    If you are going to use this or a similar display, write a small paragraph for publication in the bulletin describing the symbolism employed.

VISUAL RESOURCES
• Fabric: Ten yards purple cotton, purchased at a local fabric store
• Purple pillar candles, purchased at a local craft store
• Brass cross, from the vestibule of St. Paul's UMC
• Rocks, plant stands, and jade plant, borrowed from Jerry and Barbara Popp, members of the visual arts team
• Other plants, borrowed from Bud's Florist and Greenhouse

WORSHIP RESOURCES
"Hungry," DMC songbook, p. 43 and CD, disc A. See also WOW Orange songbook, p. 63 and CD, orange disc; or iWOR multiformat trax.

"In the Light," DC Talk, *Intermission: The Greatest Hits* CD (ForeFront Records).

"Lead Me, Guide Me," TFWS, no. 2214.

"Lord, Have Mercy," WA songbook, p. 31 and CD. Solo tracks available from Provident Music Distribution.

"Lord, Reign in Me," DMC songbook, p. 61 and CD, disc A. See also WOW Green songbook, p. 94 and CD, disc 1; and Jami Smith's *Home* CD available from Vertical Music.

The Lion, the Witch, and the Wardrobe, the first film in the BBC's *The Chronicles of Narnia* series, available on DVD and VHS from Home Vision Entertainment.

"Walkin' Through the Wilderness," a jazzy call and response song by Nylea L. Butler-Moore. For more information, contact nbmoosic@aol.com.

"Your Name Is Holy," DMC songbook, p. 94 and CD, disc A.

ADDITIONAL RESOURCES

"Change My Heart, O God," TFWS, no. 2152. See also DMC songbook, p. 13 and CD, disc B; MGB, no. 16; or WOW Blue songbook, p. 20 and CD, yellow disc.

"Draw Me Close," DMC songbook, p. 24 and CD, disc A.

"Light of the World," TFWS, no. 2204.

"Light the Fire Again," DMC songbook, p. 58 and CD, disc A. See also WOW Orange songbook, p. 116 and CD, orange disc.

"Nothing Can Trouble," TFWS, no. 2054.

Prayers in UMH: "For Guidance," no. 366; "For True Life," no. 403; "The Sufficiency of God," no. 495, "A Covenant Prayer in the Wesleyan Tradition," no. 607.

"Refiner's Fire," DMC songbook, p. 69 and CD, disc A. See also WOW Blue songbook, p. 121 and CD, yellow disc.

"Song of the Temptation," words by Sylvia G. Dunstan and music by David Haas (GIA Publications, Inc.), unison voices, guitar, and keyboard. See also David Haas, *Before I Was Born* (GIA Publications, Inc.), collection available on CD and cassette.

"Take My Life," DMC songbook, p. 76 and CD, disc B. See also WOW Blue songbook, p. 131 and CD, blue disc.

"The Change," by Steven Curtis Chapman, *Speechless* songbook (Hal Leonard Corporation); CD available from Sparrow; solo tracks available from Praise Hymn Soundtracks.

Kicking the Habit

Musical Invitation *(Worship Music Leaders)*

Songs: "Lord, Reign In Me" by Brenton Brown
"Your Name Is Holy" by Brian Doerksen

Greeting and Opportunities for Service

Song: "Lead Me, Guide Me" by Doris Akers

Video Clip from *The Lion, the Witch, and the Wardrobe*

Prayer Time

Song: "Lord, Have Mercy" by Steve Merkel

Scripture Reading: Matthew 4:1-11

Song: "Walkin' Through the Wilderness" by Nylea L. Butler-Moore

"Phone Call from Boss Diablo" *(Skit)*

Message

Song: "In the Light" by Charlie Peacock *(Worship Music Leaders)*

Offering: "Hungry" by Kathryn Scott

Sending Forth

10. Coming Home

(Palm/Passion Sunday)

Musical Invitation *(Worship music leaders may sing/play "Celebrate Love," "Hosanna! Hosanna!" or an appropriate selection of their choosing. For an excellent keyboard piece that can include other instruments, consider Craig Curry's arrangement of "All Glory, Laud, and Honor." See Additional Resources below.)*

Greeting and Opportunities for Service

Call to Worship
L: Rejoice! The gates of hope are thrown open for us!
P: Hosanna! This is a great day!
L: Let's enter to praise God's marvelous works and celebrate God's presence with us.
P: Hosanna! God's Son is coming to save us. God will triumph at last!
L: God's steadfast love endures forever!
P: Hosanna! Praise be to God!

Songs: "Celebrate Love," TFWS, no. 2073
   "Praise the Name of Jesus," TFWS, no. 2066

"Parade Preparations" *(Skit)*
(For two actors, male or female)

Speaker 1: I think I've got everything.

Speaker 2: From the looks of things, you bought out the Big Party Store! What did you get?

Speaker 1: Hundreds of helium-filled balloons, thousands of curly streamers, confetti, signs saying, "Welcome to the King." Did I forget anything?

Speaker 2: What else is there?

Speaker 1: We'll have ten floats featuring some of the highlights of his wonderful reign. Maybe I should get bands from the local youth organizations, majorettes, and flag twirlers to accompany the floats.

Speaker 2: Sounds like a great idea! Do you think the King will stop at the reviewing stand to make a speech?

Speaker 1: Yes, but if not, that's been taken care of. We've arranged a laser light display so everyone can see his face, up in lights!

Speaker 2: This is the day we've been waiting for—the King finally arrives! Things will be different once he sets foot in the city.

Speaker 1: You bet they will! No more political hacks to badger us. The King will get rid of all those people. Best of all, we'll be in control of our country again.

Speaker 2: Well, I've got to get going. The refreshment area is starting to fill up with people, and I need to check the booths. I'm the official "taste-tester," you know.

Speaker 1: See you after the parade!

Processional Song: "Hosanna! Hosanna!" TFWS, no. 2109 *(See also CC.)*

(If you want children to process with palms, they may enter at this time, placing their palm branches in containers at the front of the worship space.)

(If this is a new song for your congregation, teach the congregation the initial "Hosanna, Hosanna" portions only. Every time those words are proclaimed, the congregation should sing them. Invite the children to lead the "Hosanna" passages.)

Responsive Scripture Reading: John 12:13b-16

(Using a transparency, or PowerPoint or other projection software/equipment, project a graphic of palm branches or Jesus entering Jerusalem on a donkey.)

P: *(Shout!)* Hosanna! Blessed is the One who comes in the name of the Lord—the King of Israel!
L: Jesus found a young donkey and sat on it.
   As it is written: "Do not be afraid, Daughter of Zion.
   Look, your king is coming sitting on a donkey's colt!"
   His disciples did not understand these things at first,
   but when Jesus was glorified,
      then they remembered that these things had been written of him and had been done to him.

Sung Response: "Hosanna! Hosanna!" TFWS, no. 2109 *(Two refrains)*

Prayer

Comforting God, it is easy to lose ourselves
    in the shouts of welcome on this day.
We raise our palms and cry: "Blessed is the One
    who comes in the Name of the Lord."
We want the peace and joy that was proclaimed so
    long ago at Christ's birth,
    and yet we are fully aware that there are omi-
    nous overtones to this day.
There are those who declare that love is a fantasy
    and peace cannot endure.
We live in the knowledge that love can erase our
    fears. Meet us here, O Lord. Amen.

Message Movers

Homecoming celebrations in high schools and colleges are big events. Festivities abound for the returning graduates, as well as for the students currently enrolled. Most people look forward to the fun and excitement of this traditional event. Often we think of homecomings as joyous celebrations. We are welcomed into the arms of family and friends, of memories and belonging.

Jesus' entry into Jerusalem was another sort of homecoming. This journey would be the climax of his earthly ministry. The message he was called to proclaim would reach a dramatic urgency. Hostile factions that would not tolerate unrest (the Jewish religious authorities and the Roman government) would directly affect his last days. Jesus was returning to the heart and home of the religious and political life of Israel. He was coming back home, not to be heralded as a hero, but to be among the people of God, offering the message of repentance and redemption.

Even the disciples were caught up in the joy of the moment. "Now we're in Jerusalem. The time has come when Jesus will make everything right. No more Roman rule. God's kingdom will be established right here and now." We can only imagine how their hopes and dreams spilled into the reality they were about to face.

It would be easy for us to be carried away emotionally with the joy of the homecoming celebration. Would this be all that we had hoped? We want to go away from the event feeling as if all our dreams had been fulfilled. But these are our dreams, not necessarily the plans of God.

Parties and celebrations are wonderful events in our lives. But the parade, the party, and the celebration do not go on forever. We are called to the real business of proclaiming hope and healing. We are challenged to offer the message of God's transforming love. Home is not our destination. The journey is our home. It is the place on the road of faithful discipleship and service. The party and the celebration come later with the God who calls us on the journey.

Offering: "Come and Journey with Me" by David Haas *(Worship Music Leaders)*

(See GIA anthem and CD information below.)

Prayer Time—Prayers of the People

(At the end of the prayers sing the following response.)

Sung Response: "Please Enter My Heart, Hosanna," TFWS, no. 2154
    (Stanza 2, ending 2, CODA)

"To Conquer the Fear" *(A reading with movement)*

(For three readers and Worship Leader, and optional three or more dancers/mimes dressed in albs or modest dance apparel. Mimes will move in accordance with each of the statements read and then will freeze in position until their next assigned movement. See notes on mimes and "freeze frame" tableau. For the musical bed underneath the reading/dance, play "At the Cross" by Randy and Terry Butler.)

Reader 1: Almighty God, fear eats away at our faith.

(As this phrase is being spoken, the first mime assumes tableau position, right of center in worship area—kneeling, head bowed, body positioned as though in pain.)

Reader 2: Like Peter, we swear boldly in the company of the faithful that we will never deny Jesus. Then when other believers are not around, we speak and act as if we never knew Jesus existed.

(As this phrase is being spoken, the second mime assumes tableau position, left of center in the worship area—mime stands defiantly as though daring someone to challenge him or her.)

Reader 3: Like the young man who left his clothes behind in order to escape Jesus' accusers, we are afraid of what the accusations of others might do to us.

(As this phrase is being spoken, the third mime assumes tableau position, center of worship area—bent over forward slightly with hands and arms placed in front of the face as if an attack is imminent.)

(As the next three lines are spoken, the mimes break from the freeze positions and mime the movements: Mime 1— standing strong; Mime 2— faithfully walking; Mime 3—conquering fear. When Mime 3 completes the position, the three move together, making gestures of praise to God, lifting hands upward—strong movements may be used and should continue through the Worship Leader's lines below.)

Reader 1: God, we hate the fear that makes us hate ourselves. We want to stand strong and true to our convictions.

Reader 2: Like Jesus, we want to faithfully walk the path you set, even if it means the sacrifice of our lives.

Reader 3: God, we want to conquer the fear that keeps us from honoring you.

WL: Jesus did not suffer crucifixion for saintly people. Jesus died for people like Peter, who denied him, and the young man who ran away naked, and for you and me, who are afraid to be faithful.

(Mimes may continue appropriate motions throughout the following song. If the mimes are moving during the song, they may gradually diminish their moves in preparation to leave the worship area.)

Song: "At the Cross" by Randy and Terry Butler

(Note: This song is also appropriate for a Maundy Thursday or a Tenebrae Service.)

Responsive Sending Forth
L: Jesus died so that fear can no longer control us.
P: He died so that we can be free.
L: He died so that we can walk the path God has set before us.
P: Sin is powerless. Death cannot hold us.
L: Fear's enforcers are destroyed.
P: Jesus Christ has set us free!
L: Go, and live boldly the godly lives with which we can honor our Savior and God. Amen.

(Worship music leaders may play "At the Cross" or another appropriate selection as the congregation exits.)

Service 10. "Coming Home" Visual Resources and Ideas

DESIGN CONCEPT

Palm/Passion Sunday lends itself to a variety of displays. We chose to depict a path on which cloaks and wraps are spilled for the parade of the Savior. The colors of the fabric have little significance, except that they show up well against the burlap. The candles represent the lives that Jesus touched with his healing and forgiving love. The rocks and stones represent the difficulty of the journey. Purple is the color of Lent, so it has been used throughout the season.

DESIGN AND DISPLAY SUPPLIES AND RESOURCES

Structure

Use the back tabletop riser (66" x 12" x 6"), and put two candles on it. Elevate one candle about four inches and the other two inches. Create a level of about six inches above the back table top riser for the large Boston fern. Put the milk crate at the front of the table for an extra level.

Fabric

Drape ten yards of purple cotton over the back table top riser and the table itself. "Spill" landscaper's burlap down the table. Use four pieces of fabric to represent the cloaks and wraps strewn along the path.

Candles

On the back table top riser, use two 10-inch, two 6-inch, and two 4-inch purple pillar candles.

Florals and Plants

Place a large Boston fern on the back table top riser. Directly below that position two small Boston ferns. To the right side of the table on a medium plant stand, place the large snake plant, with the smaller potted palm in front of it. To the left of the table, put the smaller snake plant on a medium-sized plant stand. The other potted palm plant and two spiky plants are in front of the snake plant.

Other Items

To create the image of fabric spilling forth, place a basket on the table. Use marble chips on the table and at the base of the table to create a sense of a rough and rocky road. Place large rocks at the base to offer a different texture to the design.

SPECIAL NOTES

Nonmovable architectural elements in your worship space can provide unique challenges. You have to work around the existing architecture. In our chancel area hangs a large fifteen-foot oak cross, and it cannot be moved. In this setting, the architecture plays an important part in the visual effect.

VISUAL RESOURCES
• Fabric: Purple cotton and the four pieces of fabric for "cloaks," purchased from a local fabric store. Fifty-foot roll of landscaper's burlap, purchased from a landscaping center
• Rocks, stones, and snake plants: Borrowed from Jerry and Barbara Popp, members of the visual arts team

- Other plants: Borrowed from Bud's Florist and Greenhouse
- Candles: Purchased from a local craft store

WORSHIP RESOURCES

"At the Cross," DMC songbook, p. 5 and CD, disc B.

"Celebrate Love," TFWS, no 2073.

"Come and Journey with Me," by David Haas, *Celebration Series* (GIA Publications, Inc.), unison voices or solo, guitar, and keyboard, with optional congregation. See also *You Are Mine,* Vol. 2 (GIA Publications, Inc.), available on CD and cassette.

"Hosanna! Hosanna!" TFWS, no. 2109 or CC, no. 45. See also Nylea L. Butler-Moore's arrangement for two-part choir, solo, keyboard and optional synthesizer (Abingdon Press); rehearsal/accompaniment cassette also available.

"Please Enter My Heart, Hosanna," TFWS, no. 2154 or CCJ, no. 1.

"Praise the Name of Jesus," TFWS, no. 2066.

ADDITIONAL RESOURCES

"All Glory, Laud, and Honor," arranged by Craig Curry, *Blue Curry* (Glory Sound, a division of Shawnee Press), sacred arrangements for solo piano with optional rhythm section; CD available from Radical Middle Music; book and CD combo pack and instrumental parts also available. (This is a great collection for the intermediate/advanced pianist.)

"Behold the King," by Joseph M. Martin (Shawnee Press), SATB anthem with piano. (This lovely anthem, suitable for a small vocal ensemble, takes you from Jesus' triumphal entry into Jerusalem to the Passion.)

"Hosanna," by Carl Tuttle, WOW Green songbook, p. 80 and CD, disc 2.

"Hosanna," from *Jesus Christ Superstar* by Andrew Lloyd Webber and Tim Rice (Universal Music Publishing Group, Warner Bros. Publications). Songbook, CD, and cassette available.

"I Come to the Cross," by Bob Somma and Bill Batstone, MGB, no. 122.

"I Don't Know How to Love Him," from *Jesus Christ Superstar* by Andrew Lloyd Webber and Tim Rice (Universal Music Publishing Group, Warner Bros. Publications). Songbook, CD, and cassette available.

"The Wonderful Cross," by Chris Tomlin, J. D. Walt, and Jesse Reeves, WA songbook, p. 18 (also on CD). Based on Isaac Watts's hymn, "When I Survey the Wondrous Cross."

Coming Home

Musical Invitation *(Worship Music Leaders)*

Greeting and Opportunities for Service

Call to Worship
L: Rejoice! The gates of hope are thrown open for us!
P: Hosanna! This is a great day!
L: Let's enter to praise God's marvelous works and celebrate God's presence with us.
P: Hosanna! God's Son is coming to save us. God will triumph at last!
L: God's steadfast love endures forever!
P: Hosanna! Praise be to God!

Songs: "Celebrate Love" by Handt Hanson
"Praise the Name of Jesus" by Roy Hicks, Jr.

"Parade Preparations" *(Skit)*

Processional Song: "Hosanna! Hosanna!" by Cathy Townley

Responsive Scripture Reading: John 12:13b-16
P: *(Shout!)* Hosanna! Blessed is the One who comes in the name of the Lord—the King of Israel!
L: Jesus found a young donkey and sat on it.
    As it is written: "Do not be afraid, Daughter of Zion.
    Look, your king is coming sitting on a donkey's colt!"
    His disciples did not understand these things as first,
    but when Jesus was glorified,
    then they remembered that these things had been written of him
    and had been done to him.

  Sung Response: "Hosanna! Hosanna!" *(Two refrains)*

Prayer

Message

Offering: "Come and Journey With Me" by David Haas *(Worship Music Leaders)*

Prayer Time—Prayers of the People
  Sung Response: "Please Enter My Heart, Hosanna" by Cathy Townley *(Stanza 2, ending 2, CODA)*

"To Conquer the Fear" *(A reading with movement)*

Song: "At the Cross" by Randy and Terry Butler

Responsive Sending Forth
L: Jesus died so that fear can no longer control us.
P: He died so that we can be free.
L: He died so that we can walk the path God has set before us.
P: Sin is powerless. Death cannot hold us.
L: Fear's enforcers are destroyed.
P: Jesus Christ has set us free!
L: Go, and live boldly the godly lives with which we can honor our Savior and God. Amen.

11. Listening for Our Name

(Easter Sunday)

Musical Invitation: "Hallelujah!" (from *Handel's Messiah: A Soulful Celebration*) by G. F. Handel, arranged by Mervyn Warren, Michael O. Jackson, Mark Kibble
(Worship Music Leaders; instruments only)

Greeting and Opportunities for Service

Call to Worship

L: Something miraculous has happened here!
P: It's hard to believe! Our fears have been banished.
L: What Jesus had said would happen, has happened! He is risen!
P: Christ is risen indeed!

Songs: "Christ the Lord Is Risen Today," UMH, no. 302
"Lord, I Lift Your Name on High," TFWS, no. 2088

African Medley: "What a Mighty God We Serve," TFWS, no. 2021 *(Stanzas 1, 2, and 3)*
"Christ the Lord Is Risen," TFWS, no. 2116 *(Choose several stanzas.)*
"What a Mighty God We Serve," TFWS, no. 2021 *(Stanza 4)*

"Jesus Calls Mary's Name" (John 20:1-18)

(A retelling of the scripture for one female actor)

Mary Magdalene: It's true—Jesus, who was crucified and buried, is risen! He spoke to me this morning at the garden tomb, and he called me by name! I'm on top of the world, and I—forgive me. I probably should give you the whole story.

Early this morning, I went to the tomb to grieve. The large stone that sealed the tomb had been rolled away. What had happened? Who had moved the stone? I was so startled that I ran all the way to the "hiding place" where the disciples were gathered.

When I told them the news, Peter and John raced to the tomb. Peter saw the burial linens lying there. Oddly enough, the cloth that had covered Jesus' head had been neatly folded and was lying by itself. Neither Peter nor John knew what to make of it. The two of them went back to their homes, and I remained behind, weeping.

When I looked in the tomb, I saw two men sitting where Jesus' body had been lying. (I later realized that they must have been angels.) They asked me why I was crying. I told them that someone had taken my Lord away and I didn't know where they had laid him.

I turned around and saw the gardener standing there. He asked me the same question, "Woman, why are you weeping? Whom do you seek?" I said to him, "If you've carried him away, tell me where you have laid him and I will claim his body."

Then it happened—I couldn't believe my ears! The gardener called my name, "Mary!" In that instant I knew that it was the Lord! I wanted to embrace him. I wanted to dance, to sing, to shout—but he said that he wanted me to go to the disciples and tell them what I had seen. So, I ran! I raced as fast as I could back to the disciples.

"I have seen the Risen Lord! I have seen the Lord!" It was true, it was all true. Just as Jesus said it would be. He is risen! He has conquered death. This has changed me; I'm different now. I'm not afraid. The Lord is risen!

Song: "Hallelujah!" (from *Handel's Messiah: A Soulful Celebration*) by G. F. Handel, arranged by Mervyn Warren, Michael O. Jackson, Mark Kibble

(Suitable for worship music leaders, SATB choir, or small vocal ensemble)

Message Movers

Many of us have memories of our mothers calling our names. When we heard our full names, we knew we were in trouble. Full names were rarely used, unless the issue was serious. When just the first name was called, things generally were okay.

Consider Karen, a child who was adopted at age nine. Upon her adoption, her parents allowed her to change her middle name. She pondered a great number of choices and finally settled on Ann-Marie. She was proud of her choice. When her daughter was born, Karen and her husband, John, selected the name Marian (in honor of John's mother who had died many years ago).

Names in our families have special meaning. When our names are called, we respond. When Jesus called Mary's name, she was no longer bound to what she perceived as the world's possibilities or impossibilities. She was free! The Christ has spoken her name. He did not say the generic "woman"; he said "Mary." This message was personal. She was connected to the Risen Lord.

We come to this Easter day, witnessing again the miracle in the garden. What was once a place of death becomes a place of incredible life. And in the midst of that life, Jesus calls our name. It is personal. We are connected to the Risen Lord. We will never be the same after this moment; we will be changed! We are not anonymous observers, we are witnesses to God's greatest gift—the fulfillment of "God-with-us." Even death could not hold Christ.

When Jesus calls our name, he does not call to scold or warn. He calls to welcome and transform our lives. Transformation is risky. We will never be the same.

Easter is not bunnies and colored eggs. It is radical transformation from death to life. We are called to believe, and in believing to go forth in the world proclaiming the good news of God's steady and unchanging love. The Savior who calls us by name goes with us. Hallelujah!

Song: "Hallelujah (Your Love Is Amazing)" by Brenton Brown and Brian Doerksen *(See DMC or iWOR.)*

Litany for Service
L: Your love is amazing to us, Lord.
    Your presence and your steadfast love
    make us strong witnesses to your resurrection.
P: Remind us, Lord, of the many ways
    you have touched and healed our lives,
    the many ways you have brought light to our
    darkness.
L: You have gathered us together and called us to be
    your church.
    We journey with you, aware of your presence
    and empowered to be your people in the world.
P: Free us from our fears, Lord. Let us, inspired by
    your love,
    be bold witnesses to your love and mercy.
L: Beyond our doors, yet ever so close to us,
    there are communities where people lead lives
    of stress and division.
    Pressures and difficulties, as well as joy and hope,
    are ever present in these communities.
P: Jesus gathered disciples, taught and healed them,
    and sent them out into communities
    to bring healing and hope, justice and
    freedom.
    Let us be people who care about our communities
    and demonstrate that caring in our actions
    through ministries of peace and justice.
L: Lord, there are many barriers erected around the
    world,
    some political, some cultural, many born out of
    fear.

You ask us to cross borders of injustice, alienation,
    and hostility,
    to bring healing and hope.
P: Stretch us, Lord, to look beyond our doors,
    our community, and even our nation,
    to places where your love, mercy, and justice
    are needed.
    Encourage, empower, inspire, and prepare us
    to be your people in this world
    as we celebrate the resurrection of the One
    who was most perfectly your Son.

Sung Response: "Hallelujah (Your Love Is Amazing)" by Brenton Brown and Brian Doerksen *(Refrain)*

Offering *(Special music by adult, children, youth, or bell choir)*

Closing Song: "Halle, Halle, Halleluja," TFWS, no. 2026-a *(Sing several times.)*

Sending Forth: *(Congregation in unison)*
We are witnesses to this incredible gift of new life
    from God.
Nothing can hold us back.
We are willing to go and help others seek God's
    amazing and abundant love and power.
    Amen and Amen!

(As the congregation exits, music worship leaders may play/sing "Halle, Halle, Halleluja.")

Service 11. "Listening for Our Name" Visual Resources and Ideas

DESIGN CONCEPT
We had a delightful time creating this worship setting. On the two signs are names of families and individuals in our congregation, as well as relatives of the design team members. As we wrote their names on the signs, we rejoiced in how they had touched our lives. White and gold are the colors of Easter. We covered the table in white and used the antique gold fabric to create a splash down the center.

DESIGN AND DISPLAY SUPPLIES AND RESOURCES

Structure
Use the back tabletop riser, plus a two-inch-high block to elevate the brass cross.

Fabric
Drape the altar in ten yards of white cotton. Antique gold lining creates a nice centering splash down the front of the table. Put white netting around the Easter plants.

Candles

Use five candles. Place two 6-inch white pillar candles on the back table top riser. Center one 10-inch white pillar candle between two 6-inch white pillar candles, which are placed on the main level of the table.

Florals and Plants

Put a large snake plant on a tall plant stand and position behind the table. Place two small Boston ferns on either end of the back table top riser. The main level of the table had the spiky plants at each end. Potted palms are placed on the floor beside the right and left corners of the table. (Because the photo for this display was taken in July, we could not get Easter plants in abundance, either natural or artificial; so, we used what we had at hand. You may wish to use real flowers, rather than artificial.) Place Easter lilies on a small plant stand. A medium-plant stands holds the daffodils. Position vases of tulips and other spring flowers in front of the lilies and daffodils. Cover with white netting to disguise the plant stands.

Other Items

Center the brass cross on the back table top riser in front of the snake plant.

SPECIAL NOTES

You may wish to add the traditional Easter plants in place of the green plants. We like the way this design turned out, although it would be gorgeous with Easter flowers.

VISUAL RESOURCES

- Fabric: Ten yards of white cotton, four yards of antique gold silkene lining, and eight yards of white netting, purchased at a local fabric store
- White pillar candles: Purchased at a local craft store
- One foam core display board cut in half: Purchased at office supply store
- Permanent markers: Borrowed from the church secretary's office
- Snake plants and plant stands: Borrowed from Jerry and Barbara Popp, members of the visual arts team
- Large plants, small ferns, spiky plants, and artificial tulips and daffodils: Borrowed from Bud's Florist and Greenhouse

WORSHIP RESOURCES

"Christ the Lord Is Risen," TFWS, no. 2116.

"Christ the Lord Is Risen Today," UMH, no. 302. See also MGB, no. 17 or CC, no. 48.

"Halle, Halle, Halleluja," TFWS, no. 2026-a.

"Hallelujah!" from *Handel's Messiah: A Soulful Celebration*), arranged by Mervyn Warren, Michael O. Jackson, Mark Kibble (Warner Brothers Music Publications); SATB, upbeat gospel style, orchestration parts for two trumpets, tenor sax, trombone, guitar, bass, and drums. See also WOW Christmas songbook, p. 74 and CD, red disc.

"Hallelujah (Your Love Is Amazing)," DMC songbook, p. 36 and CD, disc A. See also WOW Green songbook, p. 63 and CD, disc 1 or iWOR songbook, CD set, and multiformat trax.

"Lord, I Lift Your Name on High," TFWS, no. 2088. See also WOW Blue songbook, p. 87 and CD, blue disc or iWOR songbook, CD set, DVD "C," and multiformat trax.

"What a Mighty God We Serve," TFWS, no. 2021.

ADDITIONAL RESOURCES

"Gather Us In," TFWS, no. 2236.

"He Knows My Name," WOW Green songbook, p. 76, and CD, disc 1. See also iWOR songbook, CD set, and DVD "C" or Tommy Walker, *Never Gonna Stop*, p. 59 and CD (Hosanna! Music).

"Holy and Anointed One," DMC songbook, p. 40 and CD, disc B. Solo tracks available from Praise Hymn Soundtracks.

"Resurrection Medley," by Joe Cox (Abingdon Press), SATB, congregation, piano, and optional C instrument. Rehearsal/accompaniment CD also available. Suitable for use with a worship band or ensemble.

"Shepherd of My Soul," MGB, no. 65.

"Song of the Risen One" by David Haas, *You Are Mine, Vol. 2* collection (GIA Publications, Inc.). Available in CD or cassette format.

"The Lord Almighty Reigns," DMC songbook, p. 79 and CD, disc B.

"Thine Is the Glory" by G. F. Handel in *Curry and Salsa*, arranged in a cha-cha-cha style by Craig Curry (Glory Sound, a division of Shawnee Press) sacred arrangements for solo piano with optional rhythm section; instrumental parts also available. CD available from Radical Middle Music. (This is a fun collection for the intermediate/advanced pianist.)

"We Celebrate the Love of God," CC, no. 49.

"You Are Holy (Prince of Peace)," WA songbook, p. 67 and CD. See also iWOR, DVD "D." Solo tracks available from Praise Hymn Soundtracks.

Listening for Our Name

Musical Invitation: "Hallelujah!" (from *Handel's Messiah: A Soulful Celebration*) by G. F. Handel, arranged by Mervyn Warren, Michael O. Jackson, Mark Kibble *(Worship Music Leaders)*

Greeting and Opportunities for Service

Call to Worship
L: Something miraculous has happened here!
P: It's hard to believe! Our fears have been banished.
L: What Jesus had said would happen, has happened! He is risen!
P: Christ is risen indeed!

Songs: "Christ the Lord Is Risen Today" by Charles Wesley
"Lord, I Lift Your Name on High" by Rick Founds

African Medley: "What a Mighty God We Serve" *(Traditional African folk song) (Stanzas 1, 2, and 3)*
"Christ the Lord Is Risen" by Tom Colvin *(Choose several stanzas.)*
"What a Mighty God We Serve" *(Stanza 4)*

"Jesus Calls Mary's Name" (John 20:1-18)

Song: "Hallelujah!" (from *Handel's Messiah: A Soulful Celebration*) *(Worship Music Leaders)*

Message

Song: "Hallelujah (Your Love Is Amazing)" by Brenton Brown and Brian Doerksen

Litany for Service
L: Your love is amazing to us, Lord. Your presence and your steadfast love make us strong witnesses to your resurrection.
P: Remind us, Lord, of the many ways you have touched and healed our lives, the many ways you have brought light to our darkness.
L: You have gathered us together and called us to be your church. We journey with you, aware of your presence and empowered to be your people in the world.
P: Free us from our fears, Lord. Let us, inspired by your love, be bold witnesses to your love and mercy.
L: Beyond our doors, yet ever so close to us, there are communities where people lead lives of stress and division. Pressures and difficulties, as well as joy and hope, are ever present in these communities.
P: Jesus gathered disciples, taught and healed them, and sent them out into communities to bring healing and hope, justice and freedom. Let us be people who care about our communities and demonstrate that caring in our actions through ministries of peace and justice.
L: Lord, there are many barriers erected around the world, some political, some cultural, many born out of fear. You ask us to cross borders of injustice, alienation, and hostility, to bring healing and hope.
P: Stretch us, Lord, to look beyond our doors, our community, and even our nation, to places where your love, mercy, and justice are needed. Encourage, empower, inspire, and prepare us to be your people in this world as we celebrate the resurrection of the One who was most perfectly your Son.

Sung Response: "Hallelujah (Your Love Is Amazing)" by Brenton Brown and Brian Doerksen *(Refrain)*

Offering

Closing Song: "Halle, Halle, Halleluja" *(Traditional Caribbean)*

Sending Forth
We are witnesses to this incredible gift of new life from God.
Nothing can hold us back.
We are willing to go and help others seek God's amazing,
abundant love and power. Amen and Amen!

12. Sparked by the Holy Flame
(Pentecost)

Musical Invitation: "Come, Holy Spirit," TFWS, no. 2125

(Worship music leaders may sing Part 1 through one time and then invite the congregation to join in singing, or they may do the song by themselves. Sing/play the song several times, before adding the descant.)

Welcome and Worship Focus

(After welcoming the people, add a sentence or two about Pentecost. For example: "The Day of Pentecost is the fiftieth and last day of the Easter season, when the church received the gift of the Holy Spirit." See BOW, no. 405.)

Call to Worship
L: Come, Holy Spirit! Fill us with the spirit of the living God.
P: Come, Holy Spirit! Set our hearts aflame.
L: Come, Holy Spirit! Blow through us with a rushing wind that sweeps away all barriers.
P: Come, Holy Spirit! Envelop us in your love, which leaps across the boundaries of race and nation.
L: Come, Holy Spirit! Send us power from above to make our weakness strong.
P: Come, Spirit, come! Give us courage to proclaim your name.
All: Alleluia! Come, Spirit, come!

"She Comes Sailing on the Wind" *(A reading with movement)*

(For two readers, ten ribbon bearers, one dove bearer, and congregation. See TFWS, no. 2122.)

(Keyboardist plays the introduction to "She Comes Sailing on the Wind" and the congregation sings the refrain. The music to the stanzas is played under the spoken lines. See "Visual Resources and Ideas" beginning on page 61 for information on creating the ribbon and dove poles and for placement of these items in the worship space.)

   Sung Response: "She Comes Sailing on the Wind" *(Refrain)*

Reader 1 reads stanza 1.
(Two ribbon bearers enter, with the blue ribbon sticks. They move around the room waving the sticks, progressing to the front of the worship area and placing the sticks in holders.)

   Sung Response: "She Comes Sailing on the Wind" *(Refrain)*

Reader 2 reads stanza 2.
(Two ribbon bearers with the green and yellow ribbon sticks move through the congregation, toward the front of the worship area. They place their sticks in the holders.)

   Sung Response: "She Comes Sailing on the Wind" *(Refrain)*

Reader 1 reads stanza 3.
(Two ribbon bearers with the lavender and purple ribbon sticks enter. They move through the congregation to the front of the worship area, placing their sticks in the holders.)

   Sung Response: "She Comes Sailing on the Wind" *(Refrain)*

Reader 2 reads stanza 4.
(Two ribbon bearers enter with the white ribbon sticks, moving through the congregation to the front of the worship area, placing their sticks in the holders.)

   Sung Response: "She Comes Sailing on the Wind" *(Refrain)*

Reader 1 reads stanza 5.
(The dove bearer and two ribbon bearers bring in the red and orange ribbon sticks. They encircle the congregation, swirling the dove over the entire group as the congregation sings. They place the dove pole and the ribbon sticks in the holders, and then leave the worship area.)

   Sung Response: "She Comes Sailing on the Wind" *(Refrain)*

Scripture Reading: Acts 2:1-13
   (If there are several persons in your congregation who speak other languages, ask them to help with the scripture reading. Each person should translate Acts 2:17-18 into a language of his or her choice, and then memorize the passage in that language.

The participants move into place during the last refrain of "She Comes Sailing on the Wind." A narrator, perhaps Reader 1 or 2 above, reads the whole scripture. The translators stand in a semicircle directly behind the narrator. When the narrator reads verses 4-6, those in the semicircle begin softly reciting Acts 2:17-18 in various languages.

Important Notes: [1] Give the people speaking in other languages sufficient time to translate the passage into the language of their choice; and [2] practice the entire scripture reading several times prior to the service.)

Song into Prayer Time: "Anointing Fall on Me," by Donn Thomas

(Worship music leaders sing two complete times through: A-B-A-B-A. Use the "B" section ["Touch my hands"] as a solo. You may wish to invite the congregation to join on the second and third "A" sections.)

Prayer Time
   Sung Response: "Anointing Fall on Me" by Donn Thomas

(Congregation sings two "A" sections: "Anointing fall on me.")

Message Movers—Part 1
   The shock of Jesus' death and the power of Jesus' Resurrection were like an emotional roller coaster for the disciples. They had been in hiding since the Crucifixion and Resurrection. They drew strength from one another, but not enough to leave the confines of their residence. On the day of Pentecost, God's holy flames descend upon them with the sound of a rush of a mighty wind. They are transformed and boldly proclaim to all people the wondrous power and love of God through Jesus Christ. They are no longer cowering. Their boldness and confidence astonishes the gathered crowd. Cowering disciples are transformed into bold witnesses to God's absolute power and love.

Song: "Spirit, Ignite!" by Nylea L. Butler-Moore
   (Presentation piece)

Message Movers—Part 2
   Where once we feared, now we can be confident. We have no mortal enemy. God has conquered death—the Holy Spirit emboldens us to proclaim with confidence that the Spirit is poured upon everyone.
   Throughout the world, the presence of God is being made known. In acts of kindness, in attitudes filled with respect and compassion—God calls us to speak out in the language of hope, forgiveness, and reconciliation to a world in which the rhetoric is war and dehumanization of people.

Response: "Spirit, Ignite!" by Nylea L. Butler-Moore

(Begin playing at the instrumental break before the bridge. Sing from the bridge to the end, with the congregation singing the echoes. Make sure one or more strong singers lead the congregation part.)

Segue into Opportunities for Service
Just think about what can happen
      when we are touched by the Holy Spirit!
Healing, hope, and joy will abound.
      God calls us to rise up and celebrate all the
      opportunities for service.
The call of God burns brightly within us.
      We can no longer be still!
Where will the call to service lead you?
      Perhaps through avenues of service here within
      this church, in the community, in the world!
Can you hear it? Can you feel it? Let God's Spirit
      ignite in you!

Opportunities for Service

Offering/Closing Song: "I'm Gonna Sing When the Spirit Says Sing" *(Traditional spiritual)*

(A B-flat major version of this song is found in UMH, no. 333. However, it works better for band and guitar in G major; see Songs of Zion, no. 81. Play in a relaxed, bluesy style, preferably with prominent lead guitar lines. Repeat as necessary until the offering is collected. Then ask the congregation to stand and sing.)

Sending Forth
Awesome Spirit, whose wind and fire
      turned frightened people into bold disciples,
      you have come among us today and filled us with
      your fire
so that we may confidently go forth to proclaim
      your powerful presence with us.
Pentecost has come again in this gathering of people.
Inspire us to witness to your love.
Give us courage to speak of your deeds of power
      and to take risks of daring discipleship. Amen.

(Worship music leaders may play "I'm Gonna Sing When the Spirit Says Sing" or "Spirit, Ignite!" as the congregation exits.)

Service 12. "Sparked by the Holy Flame" Visual Resources and Ideas

DESIGN CONCEPT
   This setting is created during the worship service. Ribbon bearers bring the ribbon poles into the service during the singing of "She Comes Sailing on the Wind." Portions of the song refer to Creation and the gift of Christ and the Holy Spirit to the world. The ribbon bearers wave the ribbons back and forth across the congregation and then place

the poles in a holder, beginning with the purple/blue ribbon poles and ending with the red poles and the dove pole.

DESIGN AND DISPLAY SUPPLIES AND RESOURCES

Structure

Construct two frames and spray paint them red to cover the two ribbon fans. Two long pole holders run along each side of the table. (Originally these were used for a large table top display, but by placing duct tape around the base of the five-foot-high PVC poles, they fit into the floor holders.) To create the dove pole, run a string through a very thin PVC pipe and attach it to the dove. Construct the dove out of cardboard and cover with felt. Secure the dove pole in a holder behind the table.

Fabric

Use a red tablecloth or piece of fabric. If you desire, create a table panel from room darkening fabric and acrylic paints. Feature the Pentecost flames in the design.

Candles

If your church has communion candles, use them on the main level of the table.

Florals and Plants

Place two large and two small Boston ferns on the floor in front of the table. Put a large leafy plant in the table center, toward the back.

Other Items

Create ribbon poles from five-foot lengths of one-inch PVC pipe. Use two 9-inch electric fans on stands, preferably positioned to blow directly upward. Attach red and yellow curling ribbon to the fan grids, and when the fans blow air through the ribbons, it will look like flames.

SPECIAL NOTES

This display takes a great deal of work, but it is worth it. The effect is dramatic. The flame panel can be rolled up and stored easily. Ribbons can be rolled around the poles and stored in a large upright box. To prevent the "flame" ribbons from getting stuck in the fan blades, put a thin layer of cheesecloth over the fan and string the ribbons through the cloth.

VISUAL RESOURCES

- Fabric: Red tablecloth, borrowed from Nancy Townley
- Pentecost flame panel: Created and borrowed from Nancy Townley
- PVC pipe: Purchased at a home improvement center
- Ribbon poles: Created by Barbara Popp and Nancy Townley
- Plants: Borrowed from Bud's Florist and Greenhouse
- Altar candles: Borrowed from St. Paul's UMC
- Fans: Some purchased from a home improvement center; one borrowed from Jerry Popp, member of the visual design team, one borrowed from Nancy Townley
- Fan frames: Created by Jerry Popp
- Dove: Created for a confirmation project at St. Paul's UMC

WORSHIP RESOURCES

"Anointing Fall on Me," CC, no. 57.

"Come, Holy Spirit," TFWS, no. 2125.

"She Comes Sailing on the Wind," TFWS, no. 2122.

"Spirit, Ignite!" an upbeat pop/rock song by Nylea L. Butler-Moore. Lead sheet available. For information, contact Nylea Butler-Moore at nbmoosic@aol.com.

"I'm Gonna Sing When the Spirit Says Sing," UMH, no. 333. See also Songs of Zion (Abingdon Press), no. 81.

ADDITIONAL RESOURCES

"Breathe," DMC songbook, p. 9 and CD, disc A. See also WOW Green songbook, p. 20 and CD, disc 1; iWOR songbook, CD set, DVD "E," and multiformat trax.

"Catch the Spirit," CC, no. 56.

"Come, Holy Spirit," MGB, no. 99.

"Let the River Flow," DMC songbook, p. 54 and CD, disc A. See also iWOR songbook, CD set, and multiformat trax.

"Lord, Listen to Your Children Praying," TFWS, no. 2193.

Prayers in UMH: "An Invitation to the Holy Spirit," no. 335; "Day of Pentecost," no. 542; "For Renewal of the Church," no. 574.

"Send Us Your Spirit," by David Haas (GIA Publications, Inc.), arrangement for choir, cantor, congregation, guitar, and keyboard with optional C instruments. Also available on CD or cassette in the To Be Your Bread collection.

"Spirit Blowing Through Creation," CC, no. 58.

"Spirit of God," TFWS, no. 2117.

"Wind of the Spirit," CC, no. 55.

Sparked by the Holy Flame

Musical Invitation: "Come, Holy Spirit" by Mark Foreman

Welcome and Worship Focus

Call to Worship
L: Come, Holy Spirit! Fill us with the spirit of the living God.
P: Come, Holy Spirit Set our hearts aflame.
L: Come, Holy Spirit! Blow through us
     with a rushing wind that sweeps away all barriers.
P: Come, Holy Spirit! Envelop us in your love,
     which leaps across the boundaries of race and nation.
L: Come, Holy Spirit! Send us power from above to make our weakness strong.
P: Come, Spirit, come! Give us courage to proclaim your name.
All: Alleluia! Come, Spirit, come!

"She Comes Sailing on the Wind" *(A reading with movement)*

   Sung Response: "She Comes Sailing on the Wind" by Gordon Light *(Refrain)*

Scripture Reading: Acts 2:1-13

Song into Prayer Time: "Anointing Fall on Me" by Donn Thomas

Prayer Time

   Sung Response: "Anointing Fall on Me" by Donn Thomas

Message—Part 1

Song: "Spirit, Ignite!" by Nylea L. Butler-Moore *(Worship Music Leaders)*

Message—Part 2

Response: "Spirit, Ignite!" by Nylea L. Butler-Moore *(Congregation sings the echoes.)*

Opportunities for Service

Offering/Closing Song: "I'm Gonna Sing When the Spirit Says Sing" *(Traditional spiritual)*

Sending Forth

13. Requirements for Successful Living

(Peace with Justice Sunday/Human Relations Sunday)

Musical Invitation *(Worship music leaders may play/sing any of the songs listed below, or an appropriate selection of their choosing.)*

Welcome and Greeting One Another

Songs: "Great Is the Lord," by Michael W. Smith and Deborah D. Smith, TFWS, no. 2022 (D major) *(For arrangements in C major, see WOW Green songbook and CD.)*

"Rise Up and Praise Him" by Paul Baloche and Gary Sandler *(See WOW Green songbook and CD or iWOR.)*

Opening Prayer: *(Unison)*
In all the earth, there is no one who compares to
   you, O God.
You are loving and just, compassionate and powerful,
   overflowing with grace and mercy.
You are our Mother and Father,
   and we come to you as children.
Be with us as we learn to see with new eyes,
   hear with new hearts, and treat you and one
   another in a new way.

Song: "Woke Up This Morning," TFWS, no. 2082

(This fun spiritual works particularly well at the very beginning of a service, as an introit sung by a small a cappella group.)

Worship Focus: *(Worship Leader)*
What is justice, and how does it affect our lives and
   our living?
Scripture and our faith tradition reveal that God's
   love for the world
is an active and engaged love, a love seeking justice
   and liberty.
We cannot just be observers.
We are called to care enough about people's lives
   to risk interpreting God's love, to take a stand,
   to respond, no matter how controversial or complex that response may be.

Scripture: Micah 6:1-8 *(Worship Leader)*

Song: "What Does the Lord Require of You," TFWS, no. 2174

(Sing the individual parts alone—Part 1, measures 1-8; Part 2, measures 9-16; Part 3, measures 17-24. Repeat.)

Witness of Service

(There are probably many persons in your congregation who are living out Micah 6:1-8. Use this time to highlight the work of these people and to recognize them in the worship service. See the following story for an example.)

Some say Micah 6:8 sums up the teachings of the Bible. There are many in our congregation who not only recognize these words, but live by them. Alan and Suzanne Metzger are two such individuals. They have a humble ministry, which incorporates justice and loving-kindness. Have you ever noticed the blue plastic bin in the cloak room at church? Sometimes it's filled with empty soda bottles, and sometimes it's empty. The Metzgers take the returnables back to retrieve the deposits, which they then combine with coupons to purchase boxed cereals for the Anchor, our local food pantry. Alan and Suzanne have provided this ministry for years now, quietly redeeming empties for those who deposit them in the bin, and multiplying the bounty for the hungry. They have given new meaning to the words, "reuse and recycle," and put into action the words, "do justice, love kindness, and walk humbly with your God." Surely God smiles on you, Alan and Suzanne. May you continue to walk in God's grace and peace.

(Reprinted from The Messenger, *the newsletter of St. Paul's United Methodist Church, Castleton, New York. Used by permission.)*

Song: "What Does the Lord Require of You," TFWS, no. 2174

(Sing the song as written, in canon. Parts may be assigned as suggested in the music, or you may divide the congregation into the three parts. Consider having one vocal leader for each of the three parts.)

Prayer Time

(Worship leader calls for the prayers of the people.)

Litany of Confession

(Ask someone in your congregation to write a litany of confession that focuses on current issues or specific concerns within your community, nation, or the world. See Additional Resources for a suggested litany.)

The Lord's Prayer (TFWS, no. 2278)

(This musical setting works well with acoustic guitar and voices.)

Message Movers—Part 1

(Slides or pictures indicating violence may be flashed on the projection screen.)

To the casual observer, the American culture is an angry culture. Look at the popular films and music that are paraded before us. The violence, hatred, and anger are portrayed as attitudes that must be copied.

Violence rocks the whole world. And we are placed in the middle. The impotence we feel in the face of boundless need and injustice is shown in the rhetoric of war. We would like to know how to make things better. Surely there is some formula that would work—we've tried so many different things. What does the Lord require of us?

(Fade out violent images into a scene exuding peacefulness.)

"In a Nutshell" *(Skit)*

(For four nongender-specific actors: "Voice" and Readers 1, 2, and 3.)

Voice: What does the Lord require of us?

Reader 1: How should I know? All I know is that things are difficult around here. The economy isn't doing well; there's crime in the streets, drugs, wars. I can't stand it! Where in the world is God? How can we get God to pay attention to us?

Reader 2: When I want my spouse to pay attention to me, I bring expensive gifts—lots of gifts.

Reader 3: I suppose I could offer God the newest SUV in my garage! It's a beaut! Got all the bells and whistles —God would certainly be "King of the Road" in that baby! Heh, heh, heh!

Reader 1: I could treat God to a vacation at my time-share in Hawaii. Even God could do with a little R & R.

Reader 3: I can put some big bucks in the offering plate next week. The stock market isn't doing much anyway, and I'll get another tax write-off.

Reader 2: Let's gather as many gifts as we can, you know, primo stuff. God will be pleased that we went to so much trouble!

Reader 1: That should meet God's requirements for us.

Reader 2: Let's get at it! We've got a lot to do.

Voice: What does the Lord require of us? God calls us to do justice, love kindness, and to walk humbly with God. That's it, in a nutshell. How hard can that be?

Message Movers— Part 2

Even as faithful disciples of Jesus, we often wonder where God is in the process. Does God even care about what's going on in the world? Ancient theology would have us believe that troubles and war are God's way of punishing us for some wrong that we have done. When we blame God for our problems, we can escape our responsibility.

In our daily living, in a culture of abundance, what is God's word for us? The prophet Micah responded to people who sought to win God's favor by making immense offerings—thousands of rams, ten thousands of rivers of oil, even their firstborn children. Micah said that God requires nothing more or less than the following:

- **To Do Justice:** To respond to the needs of the world in ways that are just and uplifting; to eradicate prejudice and attitudes of superiority that get in the way of working together for the common good; to be an advocate for and supporter of those who have no voice; to remember that once we were no people, now we are God's people.
- **To Love Kindness:** To seek good for all; to exhibit the hallmarks of kindness (compassion, hope, love, peace, joy, patience, gentleness); to treat others as we would like them to treat us.
- **To Walk Humbly with Our God:** All that we do, we do to the glory of God and not so that we will be praised for our faithfulness.

Song: "Here Am I," TFWS, no. 2178

(If possible, use acoustic guitar only, arpeggiating the chords; finger picking rather than strumming. This song may be sung as a solo or with the congregation.)

Segue into Opportunities for Service:

What can you do? Consider helping the food pantries, the soup kitchens, the shelters, and the thrift stores. Consider volunteering in mission to build, teach, heal, and bring hope to those in need. Learn about ministries of peace and justice, and teach the children that Christ commands us to live lives of love. Look around; there is much to be done. And you are called to be part of this mighty process of reconciliation and healing.

Opportunities for Service

Offering: (*Worship Music Leaders*)

"Find a World" by Jami Smith (*See Jami Smith's live CD, Home.*)

-or-

"Another Day in Paradise" by Phil Collins (*See Phil Collins's* Hits *or* But Seriously *CDs.*)

Prayer: "For Courage to Do Justice" by Alan Paton, UMH, no. 456

(*When the offering is collected, the worship leader may read this prayer or recite other prayers as desired.*)

Song: "We Are Called," TFWS, no. 2172

Sending Forth

People of God, go forth with God's blessing.
  Go to serve others and to bring
peace and justice to the world. Amen.

(*Worship music leaders may play "We Are Called" as the congregation exits.*)

Service 13. "Requirements for Successful Living" Visual Resources and Ideas

Design Concept

When the prophet Micah explained to the people of Israel that God did not expect thousands of rivers of oil, tens of thousands of rams, or even their firstborn children, he shared that God wanted a change in attitude and action. God requires us to live lives in which justice, kindness, and humility dominate our thoughts and actions. The blue fabric naturally lends itself to the image of cascading movement of water—not rivers of oil, but waters of blessing.

Design and Display Supplies and Resources

Structure

Create two table risers for the back of the table: one about twelve inches high and the other eight inches high. The one for the candles is the higher of the two. Create a two-inch riser for the main level of the table for the small fern.

Fabric

Cover the table and all the table risers with ten yards of black cotton. Drape down the front of the

table for a dramatic effect. Cascade the blue silkene from the candle riser down onto the table and then onto the floor, "puddling" it in front of the table.

Candles

On the top candle riser at the left rear of the table, place one 10-inch and two 6-inch white pillar candles, and five 4-inch off-white pillar candles. Use three wrought-iron candlesticks in three different heights. On one of these candlesticks, we put a six-inch white pillar candle.

Florals and Plants

Place a large Boston fern on the other riser at the back of the table, right side. Below the "Justice" sign, position a small Boston fern on the table. Place an artificial arrangement of hydrangeas in front of the shortest candlestick and the other small Boston fern was placed beside this. On the left side of the table by the word "Kindness," place an arrangement of an ivy plant with dry yarrow in a woven basket. Put the tall leafy plant beside the left corner of the table and the large leafed plant in front of the table near the blue "watery" cascade.

Other Items

Cut one piece of foam core display board into three unequal sections. On the larger section, paint the word "Justice"; on the medium-sized section, paint "Kindness"; on the smaller panel, paint the word "Humility."

Visual Resources
- Fabric: Black cotton and blue silkene, purchased at a local fabric store
- White pillar candles: Purchased at a local craft store
- Five off-white pillar candles: Borrowed from Barbara Popp, a member of the visual arts team
- Signs: Cut by Jerry Popp and painted by Nancy Townley
- Foam core display board: Purchased from local office supply store
- Wrought iron candlesticks, artificial hydrangea, and ivy basket: Borrowed from Nancy Townley
- Plants: Borrowed from Bud's Florist and Greenhouses

Worship Resources

"Another Day in Paradise," by Phil Collins, *Hits* or *But Seriously.* Both CDs available from Atlantic Records.

"Find a World," by Jami Smith, *Home.* CD available from Vertical Music.

"For Courage to Do Justice," UMH, no. 456.

"Great Is the Lord," TFWS, no. 2022. See also WOW Green songbook, p. 59 and CD, disc 2.

"Here I Am," TFWS, no. 2178.

"Rise Up and Praise Him," WOW Green songbook, p. 104 and CD, disc 1. See also iWorship DVD, E.

"The Lord's Prayer," TFWS, no. 2278.

"We Are Called," TFWS, no. 2172.

"What Does the Lord Require of You," TFWS, no. 2174.

"Woke Up This Morning," TFWS, no. 2082. See also *Songs of Zion* (Abingdon Press), no. 146.

ADDITIONAL RESOURCES

"Alrightokuhhuhamen," by Rich Mullins, *Songs* (Hal Leonard Corporation). CD available from Reunion Records.

"Bring Forth the Kingdom," TFWS, no. 2190.

"How Shall I Sing to God!" music by David Haas, text by Brian Wren, *You Are Mine, Vol. 2* (GIA Publications, Inc.). Available in CD and cassette format.

"Litanies of Confession #1," by Holly W. Whitcomb in *Flames of the Spirit: Resources for Worship*, ed. Ruth C. Duck (Pilgrim Press), p. 73.

"Live a-Humble," *Songs of Zion* (Abingdon Press), no. 108.

"Make Me a Servant," TFWS, no. 2176.

"Micah 6:8," MGB, no 52.

"Prayer for the City," MGB, no.142.

"Prayer of Ignatius of Loyola," UMH, no. 570.

"Screen Door," by Rich Mullins, *Songs* (Hal Leonard Corporation). CD available from Reunion Records.

"Sent Out in Jesus' Name," TFWS, no. 2184.

"Song of Hope," TFWS, no. 2186.

"The Family Prayer Song," TFWS, no. 2188.

"Who Is Like the Lord," by Holland Davis, *The Best of Praise Band: Lord, I Lift Your Name on High* (Maranatha!), CD, disc 2.

Requirements for Successful Living

Musical Invitation *(Worship Music Leaders)*

Welcome and Greeting One Another

Songs: "Great Is The Lord" by Michael W. Smith and Deborah D. Smith
"Rise Up and Praise Him" by Paul Baloche and Gary Sandler

Opening Prayer *(Unison)*
In all the earth, there is no one who compares to you, O God.
   You are loving and just, compassionate and powerful,
overflowing with grace and mercy.
   You are our Mother and Father,
and we come to you as children.
   Be with us as we learn to see with new eyes,
hear with new hearts, and treat you and one another
   in a new way.

Song: "Woke Up This Morning" *(Traditional spiritual)*

Worship Focus and Scripture: Micah 6:1-8

Song: "What Does the Lord Require of You" by Jim Strathdee

Witness of Service

Song: "What Does the Lord Require of You"

Prayer Time

Litany of Confession

The Lord's Prayer (OPPENHEIMER)

Message—Part 1

"In a Nutshell" *(Skit)*

Message—Part 2

Song: "Here Am I" by Brian Wren and Daniel Charles Damon

Opportunities for Service

Offering: "Find a World" by Jami Smith or "Another Day in Paradise" by Phil Collins
   (Worship Music Leaders)

Prayer: "For Courage to Do Justice" by Alan Paton *(South Africa)*

Song: "We Are Called" by David Haas

Sending Forth

From farewells to opportunities to serve

Genesis 12:1, 4
Ruth 1:16

14. Mobile Home

(Ordinary Time/Native American Awareness Sunday)

Musical Invitation (*Worship Music Leaders*)

(Select music that deals with journeys, such as: "People, Get Ready" by Curtis Mayfield; "The Journey" by Steven Curtis Chapman; or Craig Curry's or Eva Cassidy's arrangement of "Wayfaring Stranger." See Additional Resources below for information. If you are focusing on Native American Awareness, you may wish to play a CD recording of Native American music.)

Welcome

(After welcoming the people, offer the following segue into prayer. If you are dealing with Native American Awareness, present a worship focus about the special emphasis as part of the Welcome.)

Each of us came to this day from different
　　directions, each one set on a path seeking God,
　　discerning what it is that God would have us be
　　and do.
We come, thinking of our need for a guide
　　and a guardian on our journeys.
Let us open our hearts to God as we share this
　　prayer:

Prayer (*Adapted from BOW, no. 460*)

O God, our Guide and Guardian on the journey of
　　faith,
you have led us apart from the busy world
　　into the quiet of your house.
Grant us grace to worship you in Spirit and truth,
　　to the comfort of our souls and the building up
　　of every good purpose and holy desire.
Enable us to walk in your paths and to do more
　　perfectly the work to which you have called us.
May we worship you not with our lips at this hour,
　　but in word and deed throughout our lifelong
　　journey of faith; through Jesus Christ our Savior.
　　Amen.

Songs: "Step by Step" by Rich Mullins and Beaker
　　　(*See WA or CC.*)
　　　"Every Move I Make" by David Ruis (*See DMC or iWOR.*)

Message Movers—Part 1

It is no surprise that we live in an increasingly mobile society. It is a surprise, however, to find people who have lived in one town all their lives, and even more of a surprise if they have lived in the same house for generations.

Moving is never easy. Much preparation is required for a move. We sort through accumulated items, selecting some things to take with us and others to leave behind. This process is always a challenge.

The thought of leaving familiar surroundings and special friends who have meant so much to us, is difficult.

Abram faced this when God called him to go to a new land. Abram went, and he found newness of life and a new reliance on God's guidance and wisdom. Ruth left her homeland to accompany her mother-in-law, Naomi, into a new life.

Every day, in our journey through life, we make decisions that help determine the direction in which we are heading. Many times, we come to the crossroads and have to choose which path to follow.

Poem: "The Road Not Taken" by Robert Frost (*See Worship Resources below.*)

(A reader, preferably positioned in the back of the worship space, reads the poem. If possible, create a graphic presentation that coincides with the poem. Play soft music in the background, such as "Continue to Be" by David Arkenstone, from Windham Hill's Communion with God CD. If you are focusing on Native American awareness, consider using some subtle Native American music in the background.)

Message Movers—Part 2

Each direction we face has certain enticements, and certain questions. We are so afraid of losing touch, of losing friends, of being resident aliens in a new land. What will this new direction offer?

"Stepping Out in Faith" (*Skit*)

(For two nongender-specific actors," Person" and "Voice." "Voice" should be offstage.)

Person: (*Looks at a map.*) You want me to take my family and move to this location? But, we've never been there before. I don't even know how to get there. Why do we need to move any way?

Voice: Trust me.

Person: When do we have to leave? My boss needs about a month's notice. Then there's the business about the kids' schooling. What about a job? I need some security before I uproot everybody.

Voice: Step out in faith. Trust me.

Person: Trust you? You give me so little information. My family, especially my husband/wife, will think I'm crazy.

Voice: I will go with you to the new place.

Person: You have always been with us, but then you've never asked us to move. This is home.

Voice: Your home is with me. Trust me and step out in faith. I have an important job for you. Your gifts are vital to the well-being of some of my children.

Person: My gifts? How can my gifts be that important? Can't you use someone else?

Voice: You are the one I want. I always pick the right people.

Person: So . . . if I step out in faith, you will be with me, right?

Voice: Of course. Are you ready?

Person: (*Pause*) Every step I take is a step of faith. I put my trust in you.

Song: "I Walk by Faith" by Chris Falson (*See WOW Orange.*)

Message Movers—Part 3

And so we step out in faith, somewhat hesitatingly, but we do step out. We don't really know where our new home will be, but we know that our heart-home is in God. Our faith needs to be grounded in God-with-us, as guardian and guide.

Each day something is new in our lives. Each day there are new challenges and opportunities, whether we stay in one place or change locations. In order to grow, we have to be prepared to say "farewell" to some of our old ways, and be ready to move toward new concepts, directions, ideas, opportunities, and risks. That requires trust.

Which way will the Lord point us—to the North, the South, the East, or the West? From each of these directions come special gifts and opportunities from God. Are we ready to explore? Are we ready for the journey?

(*As the worship leader asks the congregation to encircle the "compass" (see "Centering Ourselves" below), worship music leaders play the refrain of "Shout to the North" by Martin Smith. The music continues until all are in place around the compass.*)

Centering Ourselves: (*Adapted from BOW, no. 470*)

(*For Leader [L] and People [P]. Because the people will be facing the cardinal directions, it will not be possible for them to view their responses on a projection screen; consider printing the centering responses in the bulletin, on a bulletin insert, or as a single-page handout.*)

(*See "Visual Designs, Ideas, and Resources" below for information on how to create the compass used in the centering. Place the compass on the floor in accurate alignment with the cardinal directions; put the compass in a highly visible, open location in the worship space. The Leader must be able to indicate the directions to the congregation with his or her body movements.*)

(*Congregants are now in a circle around the compass.*)

L: As we think about our faith journey, it is important to center or orient ourselves. The apostle Paul reminds us that the center of our spiritual compass, of our lives, and of the world is Christ. As in the Native America tradition of the Lakota tribe, let us look to the cardinal directions (*indicate East, South, West, and North*). From each direction we return to Christ, the center, reminded that Christ brings healing and salvation and by God's Spirit renews the face of the earth. Let us be silent as we face our center point.

(*All persons face the center point.*)

L: Let us face east. (*All persons face east.*) From the east, the direction of the rising sun, we glean wisdom and knowledge, through desert silences and humble service.

P: Enable us, O God, to be wise in our actions and in our use of the resources of the earth, sharing them in justice, partaking of them in gratitude.

(*All persons return facing center.*)

L: Let us face south. (*All persons face south.*) From the south come guidance and the beginning and end of life.

P: May we walk good paths, O God, living on the earth as sisters and brothers should, rejoicing in one another's blessing, sympathizing in one another's sorrows, and together look to you, seeking the new heaven and earth.

(*All persons return facing center.*)

L: Let us face west. *(All persons face west.)* From the west come purifying waters.

P: We pray that water might be pure and available to all, and that we, too, may be purified, so that life may be sustained and nurtured over the entire face of the earth.

(All persons return facing center.)

L: Let us face north. *(All persons face north.)* From the north come strong winds and gentle breezes.

P: May the air we breathe be purified and may our lives feel that breath of the Spirit, strengthening and encouraging us.

(All persons return facing center.)

L: If we walked a path in each direction, the sacred paths would form a cross.

P: Returning to the center, we discover Christ, who calls us and challenges us.

Song: "Shout to the North" by Martin Smith *(Refrain)* *(See WOW Green.)*

(Worship music leaders play/sing the refrain as many times as necessary until the congregants have returned to their seats. Then leaders and congregation sing the refrain twice.)

Prayer
Lord of heaven and earth,
    Lord of the north, the south, the east, and the
    west,
you know how anxious we get
    when you call us to enter unfamiliar territory.
We would like to think that you would always guide
    us in secure paths,
    that you would always give us clear directions,
    and that we would always have a safe place to
    live.
Please give us the confidence to trust in you
    and to go wherever you lead.
Employ our lives and talents in service to you,
    that there may be hope and healing for the
    world. Amen.

Segue to Offering
Let us bring forth our offerings,
    praising God for the many ways
in which we are called to serve.

Offering: "I Want Jesus to Walk with Me," UMH, no. 521 *(Traditional spiritual)*

(One worship music leader could sing the first stanza as a solo, with other vocalists joining in stanzas 2 and 3. You

could insert an instrumental pass after stanza 3 and then repeat stanza 1, again as a solo.)*

Segue to Opportunities for Service *(Worship Leader)*

The journey of faith and discipleship offers to us these opportunities for service.

Opportunities for Service

Song: "Sent Out in Jesus' Name," TFWS, no. 2184

Sending Forth: "Beauty Is Before Me" *(From the Navajo prayer tradition by Christian Native American Women for World Day of Prayer 1981. © 1981 Church Women United. Used by permisssion.)*

L: Now, Talking God, with your feet I walk.
        I walk with your limbs. I carry forth your body.
    For me your mind thinks.
        Your voice speaks for me.
    Beauty is before me and beauty is behind me.
    Above and below me hovers the beautiful.
    I am surrounded by it. I am immersed in it.
        In my youth I am aware of it.
    And in old age I shall walk quietly the beautiful
        trail.
P: May God grant each of us the grace and faith
        to walk this beautiful trail,
    knowing that God takes the journey with us.
L: Go in peace to love and serve.

(As the congregation exits, worship music leaders may play "Sent Out in Jesus' Name.")

Service 14. "Mobile Home" Visual Resources and Ideas

DESIGN CONCEPT
When Christ calls us to go forth to serve, we may not know exactly where we are going, but we can be assured that Christ will lead us.

DESIGN AND DISPLAY SUPPLIES AND RESOURCES

Structure
Incorporate the use of the back tabletop riser to give additional height to the table. Place several blocks of wood under the fabric to support the atlas and the roadmap.

Fabric
Cover the back table top riser and the whole table with ten yards of black cotton. Anchor the display with a "Cross and Path" panel depicting a road disappearing into the distance, with the outline of

mountains and the cross. Put the panel on an artist's easel and mount the easel on milk crates and several blocks of wood to achieve the correct height. Loop tight weave burlap back toward the cross panel, so that the burlap looks like roadside dirt. Loop ten yards of green fabric back over the burlap, so that the fabric looks like grass. With this fabric, cover the rest of the black, creating the image of a road heading into the wilderness. Affix yellow ribbon to the black cloth, giving the impression of the traffic lines painted on the road.

Candles

Place one 10-inch white pillar candle on the back table top riser to the left of the cross and path panel. On the main level of the table, put two 4-inch off-white pillar candles in front of the atlas and map.

Florals and Plants

The back table top level sports a rubber tree plant and the two spiky plants. Place the large snake plant to the left of the "roadway" and a Norfolk Island pine tree in front of it. To the right of the "roadway," position a second Norfolk Island pine tree, a rubber tree plant, and an orange tree.

Other Items

Use an atlas and a casually folded roadmap in this simple display. For the "Centering Ourselves" part of the worship service, take a piece of room-darkening fabric (approximately four-feet square) and paint a compass on it. The compass is placed on the floor in front of the table, with enough room provided for people to gather around it.

SPECIAL NOTES

The Cross and Path panel gives further direction to our "roadway." It can be very tricky getting it in place, but it is worth the effort.

VISUAL RESOURCES

- Fabric: Black and green cotton, tight weave burlap, purchased from a local fabric store; room darkening canvas purchased at a home décor center
- Compass: Painted by Nancy Townley
- Ribbon road line: Created by Lesley Leonard, a member of the visual arts team
- Atlas, road map, snake plant, Norfolk Island pines, and off-white pillar candles: Borrowed from Jerry and Barbara Popp, members of the visual arts team
- Rubber tree plants and spiky plants: Borrowed from Bud's Florist and Greenhouse
- Ten-inch white pillar candle: Purchased from local craft store
- Cross and Path panel: Designed by Nancy Townley and painted by Lesley Leonard, a member of the visual arts team, borrowed from St. Paul's UMC

WORSHIP RESOURCES

"Beauty Is Before Me," compiled by Marilyn M. Hofstra, from *Voices: Native American Hymns and Worship Resources* (Discipleship Resources), p. 70. Consider other materials in the collection for this service.

"Centering Ourselves," from "Acts of Congregational Centering," BOW, no. 470.

"Continue to Be," by David Arkenstone, from *Communion with God*. CD available from Windham Hill. For more information, visit www.windham.com.

"Every Move I Make," DMC songbook, p. 27 and CD, disc A. See also WOW Green songbook, p. 41 and CD, disc 1; or iWOR songbook, CD set, and multiformat trax.

"I Walk by Faith," WOW Orange songbook, p. 78 and CD, orange disc.

"I Want Jesus to Walk with Me," UMH, no. 521. See also *Songs of Zion*, no. 95.

Prayer from BOW, no. 460, adapted.

"Sent Out in Jesus' Name," TFWS, no. 2184.

"Shout to the North," WOW Green songbook, p. 114 and CD, disc 1. See also *Revival in Belfast* songbook, no. 2, and CD (Hosanna! Music). Solo tracks available from Praise Hymn Soundtracks.

"Step by Step," CC, no. 63 or WA songbook, p. 3 and CD. See also Rich Mullins, *Songs* (Hal Leonard Corporation). CD available from Reunion Records.

"The Road Not Taken" by Robert Frost, in *The Poetry of Robert Frost*, ed. Edward Connery Lathem (Henry Holt and Company).

ADDITIONAL RESOURCES

"Come and Journey with Me" by David Haas, *Celebration Series* (GIA Publications, Inc.). Arrangement for unison voices or solo, guitar, and keyboard, with optional congregation. See also *You Are Mine*, Vol. 2 (GIA Publications, Inc.). Available in CD and cassette format.

"Cuando El Pobre (When the Poor Ones)," UMH, no. 434.

"For Direction," a prayer in UMH, no. 705.

"Guide My Feet," TFWS, no. 2208.

"Home" from Jami Smith's *Home* CD (Vertical Music).

"I Want to Follow You" by Cheri Keaggy, *There Is Joy in the Lord* CD (Sparrow). Also in OGR, p. 103.

"Just a Closer Walk with Thee," TFWS, no. 2158. For a New Orleans funk arrangement for solo piano and optional rhythm section, see Craig Curry, *Curry and Salsa* (Glory Sound, a division of Shawnee Press), p. 37. Available on CD from Radical Middle Music. Instrumental parts also available. (This is a fun collection for the intermediate/advanced pianist.)

"May You Run and Not Be Weary," TFWS, no. 2281. See also CC, no. 73 and CD.

"People Get Ready" by Curtis Mayfield has been recorded by a wide variety of artists, including Curtis Mayfield, Rod Stewart, and jazz artist Fletch Wiley. Consider Eva Cassidy's version on her *Songbird* CD, available from Blix Street Records.

"The Journey," an instrumental selection from Steven Curtis Chapman's *Speechless* CD (Sparrow Records). See also *Speechless* songbook (Hal Leonard Corporation), p. 102. For more information, visit www.scchapman.com.

"Wayfarin' Stranger," traditional spiritual arranged by Craig Curry, *Blue Curry* (Glory Sound, a division of Shawnee Press), arrangement for solo piano and optional rhythm section, p. 32. CD available from Radical Middle Music. Book and CD combo pack and instrumental parts available separately. (This is a great collection for the intermediate/advanced pianist.)

"Wayfaring Stranger," traditional spiritual arranged by Eva Cassidy, *Songbird* (Blix Street Records).

"We Will Follow," CC, no. 59.

Mobile Home

Musical Invitation *(Worship Music Leaders)*

Welcome

Prayer

Songs: "Step by Step" by Rich Mullins and Beaker
"Every Move I Make" by David Ruis

Message—Part 1

Poem: "The Road Not Taken" by Robert Frost

Message, Part 2

"Stepping Out in Faith" *(Skit)*

Song: "I Walk by Faith" by Chris Falson

Message—Part 3

Centering Ourselves

"East" Response: Enable us, O God, to be wise in our actions and in our use of the resources of the earth, sharing them in justice, partaking of them in gratitude.

"South" Response: May we walk good paths, O God, living on the earth as sisters and brothers should, rejoicing in one another's blessing, sympathizing in one another's sorrows, and together look to you, seeking the new heaven and earth.

"West" Response: We pray that water might be pure and available to all, and that we, too, may be purified, so that life may be sustained and nurtured over the entire face of the earth.

"North" Response: May the air we breathe be purified and may our lives feel that breath of the Spirit, strengthening and encouraging us.

"Center" Response: Returning to the center, we discover Christ, who calls us and challenges us.

Song: "Shout to the North" by Martin Smith *(Refrain)*

Prayer

Offering: "I Want Jesus to Walk with Me" *(Traditional spiritual)*

Opportunities for Service

Song: "Sent Out in Jesus' Name" *(Traditional Cuban)*

Sending Forth: "Beauty Is Before Me" *(From the Navajo prayer tradition)*

> *Response:* May God grant each of us the grace and faith
> To walk this beautiful trail,
> knowing that God takes the journey with us.

Permission is granted to purchaser to copy for use with worship team.

15. Breaking the Chains of Our Oppression

(Ordinary Time)

Musical Invitation (*Worship music leaders may play "Rock of My Salvation" by Teresa Muller or any other appropriate selection.*)

(*As congregants enter the worship space, ushers should give each person a small length of chain, which will be used during the "Breaking the Chains" section of the service.*)

Opening Songs: "I Will Call Upon the Lord," TFWS, no. 2002
"He Will Deliver Me" by Bill Batstone (*See MGB.*)

Call to Worship

L: Has it been a tough week? Do things seem oppressive?

P: Yes. We're tired of the stress and pressure. Where can we get some help?

L: Help can be found with the Lord. It comes to us as a free gift.

P: It would be great, even for just a little while, to feel peaceful.

L: God will give you that peace. God is not far away. God is here.

P: Lord, help us to find you in the midst of our chaos.

Worship Focus: (*Worship Leader*)

Sometimes we wonder where God is. Things can get so oppressive in our lives.

Demands pull us in every direction. Like Atlas bearing the weight of the world on his shoulders, we struggle under the pressure of everyday living.

And we want to place blame—it is the boss's fault; it is our family's fault; our culture and its requirements are to blame. Something out there binds us, chains us, enslaves us. (*Holds up a length of chain.*)

Sound familiar? We're not alone in this feeling, and we're not ever alone. When we think that we can't go a step further, there is One who is there for us.

Song: "Why Stand So Far Away, My God?" TFWS, no. 2180

(*Consider using acoustic guitar with a simple percussion part—played on congas, for example. You could add a flute on stanzas 2, 4, and 5. The flute could play the melody or a simple obbligato, such as the tenor part played up two octaves.*)

Message Movers

From an early age, Joseph knew that he was different. Favored by his aged father, hated by his brothers, he was sold into slavery. But during his time in Egypt he discovered that he had special abilities to interpret dreams. It was this ability that led him from the status of a slave to a position of power and prestige in the hierarchy of Egypt. No longer a slave, but a prince, Joseph would become essential to the economic and political well-being of the nation. As the years went by, Israel experienced a famine, and Joseph's brothers came to Egypt seeking help. Joseph, who has not seen his brothers in years, receives the surprise of his life.

We know the direction of that story. The brothers arrive and are greeted by Joseph. He says that he will offer help if they will go home and bring their father to him. They are not aware that this important official is indeed their brother Joseph. Benjamin is left with him as insurance for their return. The story is completed when the brothers, along with their father, return and the family is reunited.

We could leave the story there but one important part is left out. Captivities come in all forms, and the chains that bind us are not necessarily always visible. Joseph was a captive, both literally and figuratively. He was chained to feelings of anger and resentment toward his brothers. He was captive to his gift of interpreting dreams. What did God want him to do with this gift? Where was this God who gave such a gift and then seemed to leave him alone in his attempts to understand it?

Video Clip: *Joseph, King of Dreams*

    VHS: START—49:10. Joseph, imprisoned because of false accusations made by Potiphar's wife, cries out, "God, why are you doing this to me? Do you hear me?" STOP—53:29. Clip ends at the end of the song, "You Know Better than I." Joseph's twig has grown into a small tree.

Too many people live lives of quiet futility, not seeing or nurturing the "twigs" of hope that lie within their grasp. Their occupations provide no joy, only the promise of a paycheck and, in some cases, benefits. They are oppressed, held captive.

Our captivities are often of our own making, and the oppression which we feel is determined by our inability to hope or to believe that anything else is possible. We cry out to God in our distress—"Help us, free us, restore us to your love, O God."

We want God to appear and magically "fix" our lives. We want to know when and where God will finally free us and break the chains of our enslavement. We feel bowed down by the oppression. The greatest challenge we face is letting go of the oppression, turning it over to God, and trusting. We are always hesitant to truly let it all go.

In the most mundane or difficult of situations, we are called to rely on the sense of God's presence. God will nourish something new in our desert places. We are called to have the courage to believe and grow where we are planted, to trust that God does indeed know better than we do!

Song: "Remember Your Chains" by Steven Curtis Chapman *(Worship Music Leaders or CD)*

(See Steven Curtis Chapman's Heaven in the Real World *CD and songbook. Consider creating a slide presentation to accompany the song, especially if you are using the CD recording.)*

Prayer Time

(Include prayers for courage and hope, and prayers for ourselves and our world. Ask God to replace the oppressions that threaten us with peace and purpose.)

Response: "Rock of My Salvation" by Teresa Muller *(See MGB.)*

Opportunities for Service

Segue into Offering

God is present with us.
We are called to place our trust in that abiding
    presence and to look beyond the chains that
    bind us

to the Lord who frees us.
Come, bring your gifts to the Lord
    and be free to celebrate and rejoice in God's
    love.

Offering

(Instrumental selection, such as a version of "I Will Trust in the Lord," UMH, no. 464)

(Invite one or more instrumentalists to play an upbeat selection here. If you have children or youth who are proficient on an instrument, consider asking them to participate. "I Will Trust in the Lord," for example, would work well with piano and sax; piano and lead electric guitar; piano and MIDI organ; piano and drums; piano and electric bass; or worship band.)

Breaking the Chains

(One music worship leader begins to sing "O Freedom" a cappella.)

Worship Leader: *(To the congregation)* "Throw off your chains! Listen for the sound! Come to the table and be free!"

(Music continues, and worship music leaders come to the table, throwing their chains into a large metal wash tub. The clanking of the chains as they hit the metal bucket is critical to the overall effect.)

(Ushers indicate when congregants should come forward. If someone is unable to come forward, an usher should go to that person, carrying a small metal bucket. The person throws the chain in the bucket, and the usher throws the contents into the large wash tub.)

Song: "O Freedom," TFWS, no. 2194

(Throughout the "Breaking the Chains," the above song is sung. It should feel free, spontaneous, and improvisatory, like the call and response tradition of the slaves who toiled in the fields. When the congregation has returned to the seats, the worship music leaders alter the mood of the song by humming. During the humming, the worship leader delivers the "Sending Forth.")

Sending Forth

Our chains have been broken!
    We have been set free!
Go in joy and peace.

(Worship music leaders sing "O Freedom" as the congregation exits.)

Service 15. "Breaking the Chains of Our Oppression" Visual Resources and Ideas

DESIGN CONCEPT

So many things can enslave and chain us. We can place our trust in God in the mundane, binding events of everyday living and in the extreme times of oppression. This visual setting is a stark representation, bereft of any plants, greenery, or anything that might soften the effect. Additions are made to the display during the worship service.

DESIGN AND DISPLAY SUPPLIES AND RESOURCES

Structure

Use a short plant stand on the right end of the table. Create a set of "iron bars" to symbolize imprisonment. Place the milk crate in front of the table to be the base for the metal wash tub.

Fabric

Drape loose-weave landscaper's burlap over the plant stand and the table. "Puddle" it in front of the table.

Candles

Mount three 6-inch white pillar candles on the three wrought iron candlesticks. Place two of the candlesticks behind the "bars" at the back of the table. The remaining candlestick goes in front and to the right of the washtub on the milk crate.

Florals and Plants

No florals or plants are used in this display.

Other Items

Place an old metal bucket on the top plant stand, with several lengths of chain pouring out from it. Drape one chain across the table in a great loop on the left side. The large metal wash tub contains heavy chains and is balanced on the milk crate in front. Use rocks for accents both on the table and in front of the table.

SPECIAL NOTES

This is a dramatic display. During the worship service, congregants will "break the chains of their oppression" by throwing their length of chain into the metal wash tub in the worship setting. The sound of the metal chains hitting the metal tub can be a very dramatic reminder of the power of trusting in God to deal with our oppressions and free us from the enslavements in our lives. You may need to have help in preparing this set, because many of the larger chains are very heavy. You may be able to borrow some of these chains from your local fire department.

VISUAL RESOURCES

- Landscaper's burlap: Purchased at a landscaping center
- Three 6-inch white pillar candles: Purchased at a local craft store
- Metal washtub, metal bucket, chains, and rocks: Borrowed from Jerry and Barbara Popp, members of the visual arts team
- "Prison Bars": Created by Jerry Popp using wood and PVC pipe for the bars, and spray painting them black
- Seven-inch lengths of new, lightweight chain, one for each congregant: Purchase from local hardware stores where they often will cut them for you. (These chains will be passed out at the beginning of the worship service.)
- Additional metal buckets: If some people in the congregation are unable to come forward for "breaking the chains," the ushers will need to take these buckets to them, so that they may throw their chains into the buckets.

WORSHIP RESOURCES

"He Will Deliver Me," MGB, no. 33.

"I Will Call Upon the Lord," TFWS, no. 2002.

"I Will Trust in the Lord," UMH, no. 464.

Joseph, King of Dreams, an animated film by DreamWorks Home Video, available on VHS cassette and DVD.

"O Freedom," TFWS, no. 2194.

"Remember Your Chains," by Steven Curtis Chapman, *Heaven in the Real World* (Hal Leonard Corporation). CD available from The Sparrow Corporation.

"Rock of My Salvation," MGB, no. 63.

"Why Stand So Far Away, My God?" TFWS, no. 2180.

ADDITIONAL RESOURCES

"Always Have, Always Will" as sung by Avalon. See *WOW 2001, The Year's 30 Top Christian Artists and Songs* CD, silver disc (EMI Christian Music Group).

"Free" as sung by Ginny Owens. See *WOW 2001, The Year's 30 Top Christian Artists and Songs* CD silver disc (EMI Christian Music Group). Solo tracks available from Daywind Music Group.

"Free at Last," a traditional spiritual. See *Songs of Zion* (Abingdon Press), no. 80.

"Freedom Is Coming," TFWS, no. 2192.

"Freedom Train a-Comin'", traditional spiritual. See *Songs of Zion* (Abingdon Press), no. 92.

"I Am the Way" as sung by Mark Schultz. See *WOW 2001, The Year's 30 Top Christian Artists and Songs* CD silver disc (EMI Christian Music Group).

"If It Had Not Been for the Lord," TFWS, no. 2053.

"Shackles" as sung by MaryMary. See *WOW 2001, The Year's 30 Top Christian Artists and Songs* CD blue disc (EMI Christian Music Group). Solo tracks available from Daywind Music Group.

"The Lord Almighty Reigns," DMC songbook, p. 79 and CD, disc B.

"We Are Free," MGB, no. 162.

"You Are Mine," TFWS, no. 2218. See also David Haas, *You Are Mine*, Vol. 2 (GIA Publications, Inc.). CD or cassette format available.

Breaking the Chains of Our Oppression

Musical Invitation *(Worship Music Leaders)*

Opening Songs: "I Will Call Upon the Lord" by Michael O'Shields
"He Will Deliver Me" by Bill Batstone

Call to Worship

L: Has it been a tough week? Do things seem oppressive?
P: Yes. We're tired of the stress and pressure. Where can we get some help?
L: Help can be found with the Lord. It comes to us as a free gift.
P: It would be great, even for just a little while, to feel peaceful.
L: God will give you that peace. God is not far away. God is here.
P: Lord, help us to find you in the midst of our chaos.

Worship Focus

Song: "Why Stand So Far Away, My God?" by Ruth Duck

Message

   Video Clip: *Joseph, King of Dreams*

Song: "Remember Your Chains" by Steven Curtis Chapman

Prayer Time

   Response: "Rock of My Salvation" by Teresa Muller

Opportunities for Service

Offering: *(Instrumental selection)*

Breaking the Chains

   Song: "O Freedom" *(Traditional spiritual)*

Sending Forth

Permission is granted to purchaser to copy for use with worship team.

16. Just an Ordinary Day

(Ordinary Time/Thanksgiving)

Musical Invitation (*Worship music leaders may play any of the songs listed below or a selection of their choosing.*)

"A Good Beginning" (*Skit*)

(*For two actors, either male or female.*)

Speaker 1: Whatcha doin'?

Speaker 2: Nothin' much. What are you doin'?

Speaker 1: Lookin' around.

Speaker 2: Lookin' at what?

Speaker 1: These incredible people. Each one of them is here looking for something special.

Speaker 2: Hmm . . . What do you think they want to find here?

Speaker 1: I don't know. Maybe friendship, maybe hope.

Speaker 2: Maybe they're here out of habit.

Speaker 1: I know why I'm here!

Speaker 2: I suppose you're going to tell me why.

Speaker 1: I sure am. I want to look at life a little differently. You know, look around at the world. Check out the beauty of it all. For instance, have you ever taken time to look at a leaf?

Speaker 2: OK, I'll play. What kind of leaf? A large leaf, a small leaf?

Speaker 1: It doesn't really matter; all leaves are awesome, part of God's creation.

Speaker 2: I was afraid of that.

Speaker 1: Of what?

Speaker 2: That you would get around to "God." God always seems to creep into your conversation, like God is your friend or teacher, or artist, or dreamer, or something . . .

Speaker 1: I guess that's true; God is all that and more. . . . Today I was thinking of God as creator. We see the beauty of God's creation not only in nature, but also in the people we meet.

Speaker 2: (*Sarcastically*) You mean, like in these people here?

Speaker 1: Exactly. Take that person over there—what a great smile!

Speaker 2: It does light up this room.

Speaker 1: Ever noticed the facial expressions of people when they greet each other in the worship service?

Speaker 2: No, but now that you've mentioned it, I'll pay more attention.

Speaker 1: Each person is a special creation to God, as intricate as a leaf, as dynamic as the waterfalls and mountains.

Speaker 2: Okay, okay, I get the picture. God's creation is complex and wonderful. Beauty is all around us, if we open our eyes and look for it.

Speaker 1: Yes! "This is the day the Lord has made. Let us be glad and rejoice in it!"

Welcome and Greeting One Another (*Worship Leader*)

With great joy we welcome you this morning.
Take a few minutes to greet each other,
to smile, to laugh, and to rejoice.
See God's goodness in this day and in each other.

(*To draw the people back together, begin playing "Cantemos al Señor." If possible, feature acoustic guitar and Latin percussion.*)

Songs: "Cantemos al Señor (Let's Sing unto the Lord)," UMH, no.149
"Clap Your Hands," TFWS, no. 2028 (*See also CC.*)

Prayer

Creator God, from the tiniest speck to the grandest mountain,
from the rolling sea to the limitless universe, you are with us.
In each vista we see the marks of your creative power.

Open our eyes and our hearts this day
to appreciate the incredible diversity and
uniqueness of the earth and all its inhabitants.
Help us to take time, to remove ourselves
from the rush and busyness of everyday living,
to look around and truly see the beauty.
And having seen the outer beauty of the world,
help us to see the inner beauty in each person.

Statement of Faith

(Use a statement of faith from your tradition that acknowl-edges God's act of creation, such as "A Statement of Faith of the United Church of Canada." See UMH, no. 883.)

Message Movers—Part 1

Think about what you have just read. It has to do with the awareness of God's creative energy and power and our faith as the story of God's love unfolds. What a wonderful sense of the continual creative actions of God! This is not a static faith—it is dynamic. God's time is busy!

One problem we face is the busyness of our lives. Many of us need Palm Pilots, date books/calendars, computers, or other devices to remind us of what we must be doing at any given time. Although our days are busy, we do not consider most days to be any-thing special.

The Pharisees and religious leaders of Jesus' day were also concerned with how to use time. Specific religious celebrations marked high points in time, but the rest of life/time was ordinary—without spe-cific designation.

For a moment think about your days. Do your days follow one another without moments of joy? Is life tedious and mundane? Do you mark time from one weekend to another? We often say that we live for vacations, celebrations, weekends, and breaks from the daily schedules of living. We cry, "Lord, just get us through the daily grind."

We have lost the sense of beauty in the ordinary. The tedium of our daily lives overcomes our efforts to sense God's presence with us. A friend insisted that even birthdays and holidays were nothing spe-cial: "Just another day as far as I am concerned." She found no pleasure, no wonder, no joy in her life. She was afraid to expect anything, because every time she began to hope or celebrate, something hurt or disappointed her. So to avoid being hurt, she did not invest any hope or joy in her living. But to live like that is to be immersed in continual hurt and pain. To never experience the overwhelming joy of life around us—even in the dark times, when the joy comes in the strength of family and friends—is tragic.

Has it been like this for you? Have you lost the sense of wonder? Do you long for moments of

delight and joy, perhaps like when you were a little kid lying on your back on the grass, watching the puffy summer clouds and trying to pick out various shapes?

Take a moment—look around. Nothing is ordi-nary. Each day brings wonder and delight when we take the time and accept the risk to look for it.

Many things delight me. *(Insert a personal story, using the one presented here for ideas.)* We eagerly awaited Hannah's birth. With great joy, Hannah entered the world of her mom and dad and all the people at church. What a wonder a baby is! Each day brought changes in Hannah, new discoveries and new abilities. From her first crawling ventures, to her tentative steps in walking, I watched with fascination. Each Sunday her mother or her father carried her for-ward to be with the other children for children's time in our worship service. Now she walks up front, just holding onto her parent's finger, to be with other children. She is learning and growing so fast. This time will go by too quickly. I want to hold each moment of it in my memory, to revisit the day when Hannah goes to school, graduates, and moves out into the world. What a wondrous gift it is to watch a child grow!

What surprises and delights you? Look around. God's wonders are everywhere. *(Insert a personal story, using the one presented here for ideas.)* One summer day, I stood transfixed at my office window, watching a sleeping baby fox that was curled up behind the church sanctuary. The fox awoke, stretched, looked around, and ambled back into the woods. "Thank you for this precious gift on this ordinary Wednesday," I breathed. Now, the day was no longer ordinary. I was able to see a special moment.

Song: "My Gratitude Now Accept, O God," TFWS, no. 2044
(This song could be sung by a soloist, preferably accompa-nied by acoustic guitar.)

Alternate Song Selection: "I Hope You Dance" by Tia Sillers and Mark D. Sanders
(As sung by Lee Ann Womack on the I Hope You Dance *CD)*
(You could sing this live or use the CD recording. If using the CD, consider creating an interpretive dance or a slide presentation to accompany the song.)

Message Movers—Part 2

No time with God is ordinary. It becomes ordi-nary when we fail to appreciate all that is around us and neglect the opportunities to celebrate God's love. We do not have to rely on holidays, weekends, or vacations for the source of our celebration. *(Keyboardist begins softly playing "In His Time" here.)* All time is God's time, the in-breaking, wonderful, abiding presence of creation in our midst. In the reality of calendars, watches, and Palm Pilots, may we teach our children and ourselves to enjoy the ordinary, which is after all, very extraordinary!

Segue to Prayer Time

(The keyboardist continues softly to play "In His Time" as the Worship Leader reads the segue.)

This is a time for both gathering and letting go.
   Gather your spirits to the Lord,
      let go of the stresses and struggles that you feel.
In the ordinary, begin to discover the extraordinary.

Response: "In His Time," TFWS, no. 2203

(Consider superimposing the text over graphics of beautiful scenery, followed by photos of people. The photos should reflect celebration. Make sure that the text can be easily read. After stanza 2, play an instrumental pass and then sing stanza 1 again.)

Prayer Time and Moments of Quietness: *(Worship Leader)*

(Focus on moments of quietness. Do not play any music during the prayer time because it will detract from the silence.)

Lord, help us to be quiet, to resist the desire to fill
      every moment with noise:
the noise of living, the noise of our busyness,
      the noise of plans that rumble around in our
      heads.
Clear our minds and give us a moment's peace.
(Quiet moment)

Help us to slow down enough to appreciate the
      beauty around us.
(Quiet moment)

Help us to focus on our own breathing,
      the rhythm of inhaling and exhaling,
         and to remember that you are the breath of life.
(Quiet moment)

Help us to relax in your love and creative power.
Enable us to place our trust in your abiding
      presence.
(Quiet moment)

Refreshing God, we thank you for these moments of
      quietness and relaxation.
With glad and joyful hearts, we thank you for time
      in which we can begin to experience
         the uniqueness of all creation and of each
         moment in time. Amen.

Song: "Give Thanks," TFWS, no. 2036

Segue into Opportunities for Service:

In appreciation for the joy of each day,
      we celebrate the many ways we can serve the Lord.

Opportunities for Service

Segue to Offering

What a great day to be together, to share, and to
      rejoice.
God calls us into community, to offer our gifts and
      our service for healing,
         renewal, and hope in this world.
Bring now your offerings to God in thanksgiving
      for all the incredible blessings in your life.

Offering: "Joyful, Joyful/Praise God" arranged by Nylea L. Butler-Moore

Sending Forth

Look around at each other again. Smile.
      Look with love and wonder.
Each one of us is a unique creation of God—
      there is no ordinary person here.
We are all extraordinary because God has called us so.
Go forth to discover the wonders of the world,
      and know that you are part of those joyful
      wonders.
Go out with joy and be led forth with peace.

Closing Song: "The Trees of the Field," TFWS, no. 2279

(Worship music leaders may play "The Trees of the Field" as the congregation exits.)

Service 16. "Just an Ordinary Day" Visual Resources and Ideas

DESIGN CONCEPT

This can be a dual use service, for Ordinary Time or Thanksgiving. (Photo #16 in the insert shows a visual setting for Ordinary Time.)

How often do we take the world, our families, and friends for granted? We think that almost everything in our lives is "ordinary." In this service, we want to celebrate the "extraordinary" that we have called ordinary.

DESIGN AND DISPLAY SUPPLIES AND RESOURCES

Structure

Place a large plant stand behind the table to hold the large Boston fern. Place a ten-inch-high riser at the back of the table, adding candles on this riser. To house the other large Boston fern, put a milk carton at the front of the table.

Fabric

Cover the table with ten yards of green cotton fabric. Using about six yards of antique gold silkene lining, drape the table and "puddle" the material over the milk crate. Place a hand-made doily on the left side of the table.

Candles

Use three wrought iron candlesticks, place a 6-inch white pillar candle on each of the stands. On the riser at the back of the table, place one 10-inch, two 6-inch, and four 4-inch white pillar candles.

Florals and Plants

On a large plant stand in back of the table to the right, place a large Boston fern. Put two potted palms in medium-sized plant stands and locate on the back corners, right and left, of the table. Position a large leafy plant in front of the palm plant on the left of the table. Beside this plant, add a basket containing artificial ivy. A rubber tree plant is on the right side of the other large Boston fern. Use a milk crate as the base for the large Boston fern. To the right of the Boston fern, place a rubber tree plant, and behind the medium-sized wrought iron candlestick, put the artificial hydrangea. Add a basket of artificial crocus plants in the center back of the table.

Other Items

Position a host of wonderfully framed photos across the altar. (Most of these photos can be borrowed from the visual arts team.) Try to collect photos from members of your congregation for the table. If you are going to use photos from the congregation, be sure to list the donors in the bulletin.

SPECIAL NOTES

People in your congregation will enjoy coming up after the worship service to look closely at the photographs. Be sure to return the photographs to the donors promptly.

VISUAL RESOURCES
- Fabric: Green cotton fabric and antique gold silkene lining, purchased at a local fabric store
- Doily: Borrowed from a Bible stand at St. Paul's UMC
- Candles: Purchased at a local craft store
- Wrought iron candlesticks and artificial plants: Borrowed from Nancy Townley
- Large plants: Borrowed from Bud's Florist and Greenhouse
- Photographs: Provided by Jerry and Barbara Popp, Lesley Leonard, and Nancy Townley

WORSHIP RESOURCES

"Cantemos al Señor (Let's Sing Unto the Lord)" UMH, no. 149.

"Clap Your Hands," TFWS, no. 2028; or CC, no. 70.

"Give Thanks," TFWS, no. 2036. See also OGR, p. 52; or WOW Blue songbook, p. 41 and CD, yellow disc.

"I Hope You Dance," sung by Lee Ann Womack on *I Hope You Dance* (MCA Nashville Records). Sheet music for piano/vocal/guitar published by Hal Leonard Corporation.

"In His Time," TFWS, no. 2203. See also MGB, no. 45; or WOW Blue songbook, p. 60 and CD, yellow disc.

"Joyful, Joyful/Praise God," an upbeat arrangement by Nylea L. Butler-Moore of "Joyful, Joyful, We Adore Thee" and the OLD 100th doxology. Lead sheet available. For information, contact Nylea at nbmoosic@aol.com.

"My Gratitude Now Accept, O God," TFWS, no. 2044.

"(A) Statement of Faith of the United Church of Canada," UMH, no. 883.

"The Trees of the Field," TFWS, no. 2279.

ADDITIONAL RESOURCES

"Beautiful Moments," sung by Jami Smith on her *Home* CD (Vertical Music). For more information, visit www.jamismith.com.

"Blessed," sung by Martina McBride on her *Greatest Hits* CD (RCA Records).

"Every Season," sung by Nichole Nordeman. See *WOW 2001, The Year's 30 Top Christian Artists and Songs* CD (EMI Christian Music Group), silver disc. Solo tracks available from Christian World.

"God of Wonders," iWOR songbook, CD set, DVD-B, and multiformat tracks. Sung by City on a Hill. See *WOW 2001, The Year's 30 Top Christian Artists and Songs* CD (EMI Christian Music Group), blue disc.

"God the Sculptor of the Mountains," TFWS, no. 2060.

"Let All Things Now Living," TFWS, no. 2008.

"Lord, We Come to Ask Your Blessing," TFWS, no. 2230.

"May You Run and Not Be Weary," TFWS, no. 2281. See also CC, no. 73 and CD.

Prayers in UMH: "Prayer to the Holy Spirit," no. 329; "Bread and Justice" no. 639; and "For a New Day," no. 676.

"Thank You, Lord," UMH, no. 84.

"This Good Day," sung by Fernando Ortega. See *WOW 2001, The Year's 30 Top Christian Artists and Songs* (EMI Christian Music Group), CD, silver disc.

"This Is the Day," CC, no. 69.

Just an Ordinary Day

Musical Invitation *(Worship Music Leaders)*

"A Good Beginning" *(Skit)*

Welcome and Greeting One Another

Songs: "Cantemos al Señor (Let's Sing unto the Lord)" by Carlos Rosas
"Clap Your Hands" by Handt Hanson and Paul Murakami

Prayer

Statement of Faith

Message—Part 1

Song: "My Gratitude Now Accept, O God" by Rafael Montalvo
-or- "I Hope You Dance" by Tia Sillers and Mark D. Sanders

Message—Part 2

Response: "In His Time" by Diane Ball

Prayer Time and Moments of Quietness

Song: "Give Thanks" by Henry Smith

Opportunities for Service

Offering: "Joyful, Joyful/Praise God" arranged by Nylea L. Butler-Moore

Sending Forth

Closing Song: "The Trees of the Field" by Steffi Geiser Ruben and Stuart Dauermann

17. Mastering the Money

(Ordinary Time/Stewardship Sunday)

Musical Invitation (*Worship music leaders may play "What Gift Can We Bring" or any selection of their choice.*)

Call to Worship

L: Rejoice, people of God, in the abundance of God's blessings.
  Look at each other, smile at each other.
  Can you see it—the bounty of God's goodness present with us?
P: We do see it—in these smiles and glances, we see God's presence.
L: What shall we do with all this bounty?
P: We shall offer it to God as part of our stewardship of all God's gifts to us. Amen.

Songs: "What Gift Can We Bring," UMH, no. 87
  (*Consider using acoustic guitar and voices only.*)
  "He Has Made Me Glad" by Leona Von Brethorst (*See MGB, no. 191 or iWOR DVD.*)

(*The iWorship version is strongly recommended—fun, upbeat gospel with celebratory graphics.*)

"I'll Buy That!" (*Skit*)

(*For one male and one female actor.*)

(*Maude and Claude are sitting in a church service. Maude is holding the worship bulletin and takes an offering envelope out of the middle of it.*)

Maude: I'm sick of it! Every Sunday I come to church, there's an extra offering envelope in the bulletin. This church is always asking us for money! What is this, worship or fund-raising?

Claude: Maude, the pastor told us that giving is voluntary. We don't have to give if we don't want to.

Maude: Well, I guess I feel a little guilty. What will people think when I don't put my money into the plate—that I'm cheap or unfaithful?

Claude: Maude, we don't give money to prove that we're faithful—we give because we want to help others. It's really no one else's business whether or not we give.

Maude: But there are so many things we still want to have, like a new sewing room, Junior's dirt bike, and your ATV. We have enough money to buy some of those things.

Claude: Good Lord, Maude, we have too much stuff already! Our house is bursting at the seams!

Maude: (*Hopefully*) We *could* look for a larger house! (*Claude frowns.*)

Claude: The other day I saw a bumper sticker that said, "Live simply so others may simply live." Maybe that's what we need to do, Maude, live more simply. We buy and buy, but those things don't satisfy us.

Maude: I'm sorry. I get caught up in the American dream of buying everything I want. (*Pause*) What I really want is some peace, and some time with you and the kids.

Claude: Bless you, Maude. I feel the same way. (*Claude watches Maude take her billfold out of her purse.*) Could we use this money to help someone else?

Maude: Okay, here goes. (*She takes the money out of the billfold and puts it in the offering envelope.*) This is another opportunity to offer our abundance back to God's work.

Claude: I'll buy that!

Song: "We Will Not Offer You" by Dan Adler (*See CCJ.*)

Message Movers

(*Worship music leaders could play a little bit of the chorus of "For the Love of Money" by the O'Jays here, or you could use the CD recording. Then fade out into the message. See below for resource information.*)

Money moves the world. Our whole way of life is dependent upon the bottom line, and we encourage that philosophy for all nations and call it democracy.

We are so consumed with money that even our recreation is currency-driven. Look at the abundance of casinos and lotteries. For some people, gambling has become a way of weekly and, in some instances, daily entertainment.

We are mastered by our checkbooks, ATMs, and credit cards—our very lives depend on them—and the moneychangers laugh.

We claim that the love of money is the root of all kinds of evil, but do we really believe that? When a young lad in a confirmation class was asked what he would ask Jesus if Jesus were to come through the door, his response was: "Will I have lots of money?" His wish was for great wealth, so that he would be accepted and respected.

Consider the decision made by Lester in Shel Silverstein's poem from *Where the Sidewalk Ends*. (See *Additional Resources* below.)

(Ask a congregant to present the poem. Consider creating a slide presentation to accompany the reading.)

Will our wish for great monetary wealth control us until, like Lester, we are found dead in a heap of wishes, no wishes missing?

Shall our money master us or shall we find ways to use our abundance in the service of others for the sake of our Lord? That's our challenge and our opportunity. It's our choice and our consequence.

Song: "Lord, We Come to Ask Your Blessing," TFWS, no. 2230

(Consider playing an instrumental pass between stanzas 2 and 3. If possible, vary the accompaniment slightly for each stanza.)

Segue into Offering

God's abundance is poured into our lives,
    not so we can hoard or accumulate,
but so that we may share,
    and in the sharing be part of the hope and heal-
    ing of the world.
This morning let us remember the beauty that
    surrounds us,
    the blessings that are within us,
    and the opportunities presented to us to be
    God's people in the world.
Offer to God your gifts, your love, and your life with
    great joy!

Offering: "All That We Have" by Nylea L. Butler-Moore *(Worship Music Leaders)*

Doxology: "The Doxology" by Tommy Walker *(WOW Green songbook and CD)*

(When planning this worship service, ask several persons in the congregation to think of some of the blessings and praises in their lives. During the interludes of "The Doxology," have these persons quickly express their thanks to God for these

blessings and praises. Encourage the speakers to include ways these blessings are shared with others. For example, we receive blessings so that we may be a blessing. To accommodate more share time, you can omit the vocal part in measures 35-37, 39-41, 42-46, and 48-50.)

Prayer Time

(The Worship Leader [WL] offers the following prayer sections. The congregation responds by singing "More Precious than Silver.")

WL: Lord, you are more precious to us than all the riches of the world. Riches are transitory, but your love is steadfastly with us all our lives. You offer to us an incredible world full of both wonders and problems. While we feast, others starve; while we live in security, others fear daily for their lives; while we offer our children opportunities for growth and learning, others have no hope of giving their children more than poverty. When these problems are brought to our attention, we generously offer money to help erase the problems. But the problems are bigger than our checkbooks. They require a change of heart and spirit. They challenge us to truly look at the needs of others. In addition to offering funds to help change the issues, we are called to change our attitudes.

Sung Response: "More Precious than Silver," TFWS, no. 2065 *(See also WOW Blue songbook and CD.)*

WL: Reach into our hearts this day, Lord. Remind us that you desire us to be faithful people who care more about the needs of others than chasing after the illusion of riches that the world offers. Help us to hear the cries of the poor. Give us the privilege of feeding and clothing the hungry. Challenge us to confront the systems of pain and suffering that alienate people from one another and from you, for you are more precious to us than all the wealth that can be laid before us.

Sung Response: "More Precious than Silver"

WL: Keep us mindful of all the many ways in which you have given yourself to us. Gracious Lord, we open our hearts, our minds, and our spirits this day to your word. When it is so easy for us to sit here and count our blessings, remind us of what you would have us do. Strengthen us and give us courage to be your people. Cause us to serve you in this world, which you have entrusted to us. These things and so much more that are on our hearts we offer to you in full confidence of your love and power. Amen.

Sung Response: "More Precious than Silver"

Opportunities for Service

Song: "The Spirit Sends Us Forth to Serve,"
TFWS, no. 2241

(A soloist sings stanza 1; the congregants on stage right—to the right of the worship leaders who are facing the peo-ple—sing stanza 2; the congregants on stage left—to the left of the worship leaders who are facing the people—sing stanza 3; everyone sings stanza 4.)

Sending Forth
God who has abundantly blessed us with many gifts, sends us forth to offer these gifts in service to the world.
Go in peace, and may the God of peace and hope go with you now and always.

(Worship music leaders may play "We Will Not Offer You" or another appropriate selection as the congregation exits.)

Service 17: "Mastering the Money" Visual Resources and Ideas

DESIGN CONCEPT
This was a rather difficult display to conceive. We talked about how much money seems to control our lives, rather than our lives controlling the money. We decided that we would go with a display of "money" (represented by the "gold ingots" and the "gold coins and nuggets") and placing them in conjunc-tion with the cross and the offering plates.

DESIGN AND DISPLAY SUPPLIES AND RESOURCES

Structure
Create a twelve-inch riser at the left back table-top and a six-inch riser to hold the "bucket of gold." Set the cross on another six-inch riser placed under the gold fabric. Create ingots and "gold coins" from lumber.

Fabric
Triple-layer the table with burgundy silkene lin-ing on the left, and mauve cotton on the right. Overlay the antique gold-tone silkene lining, cascad-ing it from the upper riser on the left, down across the table, and "puddling" it on the floor.

Candles
Place three 6-inch white pillar candles on the tabletop.

Florals and Plants
The twelve-inch riser holds a large-leafed plant as a backdrop for the brass cross. Place two tall plant stands for the two large Boston ferns behind the table. The large leafy plant goes on the right of the table. In front of this, set the small Boston fern. Put the artificial hydrangea plant on the left side of the table, to the front.

Other Items
The brass cross is a central feature on the left side of the table, along with two offering plates. The wooden "gold ingots" are spray painted gold, as are the coins and nuggets spilling out of the plastic "cast iron" cauldron.

SPECIAL NOTES
Check the wooden ingots and nuggets for sharp edges that can snag fabric, especially the silkene fabrics.

VISUAL RESOURCES
- Fabric: Burgundy and antique gold silkene, and mauve cotton, purchased at a local fabric store
- Artificial hydrangea: Borrowed from Nancy Townley
- Living plants: Borrowed from Bud's Florist and Greenhouse
- Candles: Purchased at a local craft store
- Cross and offering plates: Belong to St. Paul's UMC

WORSHIP RESOURCES
"All that We Have" by Nylea L. Butler-Moore, in a style reminiscent of Enya. Lead sheet available. For information, contact Nylea at nbmoosic@aol.com.

"He Has Made Me Glad," TFWS, no. 2270. See also MGB, no. 191; or iWOR DVD, disc A.

"Lord, We Come to Ask Your Blessing," TFWS, no. 2230.

"For the Love of Money" as sung by The O'Jays on *The O'Jays Collector's Items* CD (distributed by Philadelphia International Records). See also *The Ultimate O'Jays* (Sony Records).

"More Precious than Silver," TFWS, no. 2065. See also WOW Blue songbook, p. 101 and CD, blue disc.

"The Doxology," WOW Green songbook, p. 128 and CD, disc 2.

"The Spirit Sends Us Forth to Serve," TFWS, no. 2241.

"We Will Not Offer You," CCJ, no. 6.

"What Gift Can We Bring," UMH, no. 87.

ADDITIONAL RESOURCES

"Give a Little Bit" as sung by Supertramp on *The Very Best of Supertramp* CD (A & M Records).

"Give Thanks," TFWS, no. 2036. See also OGR, p. 52; or WOW Blue songbook, p. 41 and CD, yellow disc.

"I'm Gonna Live So God Can Use Me," TFWS, no. 2153.

"Joyful, Joyful/Praise God," an upbeat arrangement by Nylea L. Butler-Moore of "Joyful, Joyful, We Adore Thee" and the OLD 100th doxology. Lead sheet available. For use in this service, play from measure 17 to the end. For information, contact Nylea at nbmoosic@aol.com.

"Lester," a poem by Shel Silverstein from his *Where the Sidewalk Ends* collection (New York: Harper Collins Publishers).

"Let Us Offer to the Father," TFWS, no. 2262.

"Lord, Be Glorified," TFWS, no. 2150.

"My Gratitude Now Accept, O God," TFWS, no. 2044.

"My One Thing" as sung by Rich Mullins on his *Songs* CD (Reunion Records); songbook available from Hal Leonard Corporation.

"O God, Beyond All Praising," TFWS, no. 2009.

"Song of Hope," TFWS, no. 2186.

"Take My Life," words by Frances R. Havergal, music by Nylea L. Butler-Moore, in an upbeat pop style. Lead sheet available. For information, contact Nylea at nbmoosic@aol.com.

"Thousand Miles" as sung by Caedmon's Call on their *Back Home* CD (Essential Records). For more information, visit www.caedmonscall.com.

"Together We Serve," TFWS, no. 2175.

"Tú Has Venido a la Orilla" ("Lord, You Have Come to the Lakeshore"), UMH, no. 344.

"We Bring the Sacrifice of Praise," MGB, no. 251.

Mastering the Money

Musical Invitation *(Worship Music Leaders)*

Call to Worship

L: Rejoice, people of God, in the abundance of God's blessings.
   Look at each other, smile at each other.
   Can you see it—the bounty of God's goodness present with us?
P: We do see it—in these smiles and glances, we see God's presence.
L: What shall we do with all this bounty?
P: We shall offer it to God as part of our stewardship of all God's gifts to us.
   Amen.

Songs: "What Gift Can We Bring" by Jane Marshall
"He Has Made Me Glad" by Leona Von Brethorst

"I'll Buy That!" *(Skit)*

Song: "We Will Not Offer You" by Dan Adler

Message

Song: "Lord, We Come to Ask Your Blessing" by Fred Pratt Green and W. Daniel
Landes

Offering: "All That We Have" by Nylea L. Butler-Moore *(Worship Music Leaders)*

Doxology: "The Doxology" by Tommy Walker

Prayer Time
   Sung Response: "More Precious than Silver" by Lynn Deshazo

Opportunities for Service

Song: "The Spirit Sends Us Forth to Serve" by Delores Dufner
   Stanza 1 *(Worship Music Leader)*
   Stanza 2 *(Stage Right Congregants)*
   Stanza 3 *(Stage Left Congregants)*
   Stanza 4 *(All)*

Sending Forth

18. Friendship Cords
(Ordinary Time)

Musical Invitation: "You've Got a Friend" by Carole King

(Worship music leaders can sing this live, or play the CD recording by Carole King or James Taylor. See Worship Resources below for information.)

Call to Worship

L: We are all children of the one God.

P: We are called to worship together, to share friendship, and to support each other on our faith journeys.

L: Let us celebrate the presence of the One who calls us on the journey.

P: Let us rejoice that we have strong cords of friendship on which to rely.

Songs: "We Are One in Christ Jesus," TFWS, no. 2229

(Play in a Latin style, featuring acoustic guitar, claves, and other Latin percussion, if possible. Consider singing several times through, using both the English and Spanish texts.)

"We Are the Body of Christ," TFWS, no. 2227

Scripture: Ecclesiastes 4:9-12

Song: "In Unity We Lift Our Song," TFWS, no. 2221
(Stanzas 1 and 2)

Video Clip from *The Divine Secrets of the Ya-Ya Sisterhood*

> **DVD:** START—1:15. From the "Ya-Ya Priestesses," scene 1
> STOP—3:54.

The young girls form the "Ya-Ya Sisterhood," in which they pledge eternal love and loyalty to one another. Love and loyalty seem eternal when you are young, but can they endure the test of time?

Message Movers—Part 1

Vivian, Neicie, Teensy, and Cora banded together to form a cord of sisterhood. In their young hearts they were eternally bound together. They could not have imagined the various directions their lives would take them, but the strength of the friendship cords held strong. Through their struggles, the Ya-Ya sisters supported and helped one another. That kind of love and support was not always easy. Their strong conviction in the power of their friendship was always part of their lives, even in the willingness to risk that friendship for the sake of reconciliation between a mother and a daughter.

Friendship is a fragile thing. When we are young we have very best friends to whom we pledge eternal loyalty and allegiance. But, as we grow older, time and distance take their toll—contacts are infrequent; lives and interests change. We just don't know what to say to each other. Some friendships transcend time, distance, and changes in our lives. Sometimes we do not speak with our friends for many months at a time, but a phone call seems to erase all time and distance—we pick up right where we left off.

(Ask a member of the congregation to share a story about a special friendship here. Use the following story as an example.)

Although three thousand miles separate us, Nylea Butler-Moore and Nancy Townley have a blessed friendship. Nylea is young enough to be Nancy's daughter and yet is a special "sister" of her heart. Their love for our Lord, for music and worship, for the church and its people, and love for each other and our families, are blessed cords that bind them together. Time is erased when they converse. And when they see each other, they celebrate a special community.

One of the most critical cords is love, intertwined with forgiveness, patience, and knowledge that goes beyond what we can see. In our scripture lesson, Ruth is willing to risk her life to accompany her mother-in-law, Naomi, back to Naomi's homeland. The treacherous trip will be potentially made easier by Ruth's presence. The Lord works through Ruth's faithful love for Naomi to bring about hope. Ruth becomes an ancestor of our Lord Jesus Christ whose love knows no bounds.

Song: "I Will Be Your Friend" by Michael W. Smith *(Solo)*

(From *This Is Your Time* CD; see *Worship Resources* below).

Message Movers—Part 2

Just as God has witnessed to us eternal love through Jesus, God also offers us the blessedness of friendship through the creation of community. We are given the joy of having people enter our lives, who know us and like us just the same.

God's cord of friendship with us is Jesus Christ, who knows our joys and sorrows, who loves and listens to us, who is always there—the same yesterday, today, and tomorrow.

Song: "Hallelujah (Your Love Is Amazing)" by Brenton Brown and Brian Doerksen *(See DMC.)*

Opportunities for Service

(Lift up opportunities that bring people together—such as healing ministries; reconciling ministries through the church and in the community; food pantries; thrift shops; soup kitchens—all of which demonstrate a community of faith and friendship reaching out to the world. Some of the opportunities for service may include special groups, such as Alcoholics Anonymous, Narcotics Anonymous, bereavement support groups, and so forth.)

Offering: "More Than You'll Ever Know" by Watermark *(Friends montage)*

(Worship music leaders could sing this live, or use the CD recording. See Worship Resources below for information. Create a photographic slide presentation of congregants engaged in acts of friendship and caring. Include photos depicting diverse groups of people—young and old, different races, and people in a variety of situations.)

Prayer Time

(At the beginning of prayer time, ushers distribute one 12-inch piece of cord to each member of the congregation while the keyboardist softly plays "Bind Us Together." When the cords are distributed, the Worship Leader leads the people in the following guided prayer.)

Guided Prayer

WL: Lord, remind us that the cords of our being are formed from many single strands:
family, neighborhood, school, friendships.
Each strand by itself possesses certain strengths, but bound together they become a stronger part of the whole cord.

P: Open our memories to the many strands that make up our individual cords.

(Quiet prayer)

WL: Lord, we learn to place value on our friendships.
We do not give true friendship lightly.
Trust is crucial in our friendships, and trust is both given and earned.

P: Open our memories to the times in which friendships have been tested.

(Quiet prayer)

WL: Lord, sometimes friendships can be strained, and we long for healing and restoration, which you alone can provide.

P: Open our hearts and spirits to the need for healing and restoration in our broken friendships.

(Quiet prayer)

WL: Lord, make room in our hearts for the entrance of others yet unknown to us.
Help us to befriend them and to place a great value on their friendship for your sake.

P: Open our spirits to welcome the strangers who will become beloved friends.
Empower us to be willing to risk friendship in Christ's name. Amen.

(Following the guided prayer, the Worship Leader instructs the congregation to divide into small groups of approximately four to six people each. The keyboardist softly plays "Live in Charity" throughout this time. Have the small groups tie their cords together to create a longer strand. When each group has completed its strand, they move to the outside perimeters of the worship area. If the congregation is small, have the small groups move to the front of the worship area. As each group moves the perimeters, have them tie one end of their strand to the end of another group's strand until all strands are united in one large cord. Tie the ends of the cord together, forming a large circle.)

Song: "Live in Charity," TFWS, no. 2179

(During the tying of the cords, the congregation will sing the above song until the large circle is completed, singing the song as many times as needed.)

Unison Prayer at the End of Prayer Time

From the very beginning,
You desired community for us, your people.
You set us apart, O God,
to be mirrors of your love.
All through our life journey,
You give to us people who influence us.
Help us to be models of your love and compassion as we are in community with others. Amen.

Song: "Bind Us Together," TFWS, no. 2226

(At the end of the song, the whole group brings the large circle of cord up to the front of the worship area and places it on the communion table. Worship music leaders play the song during the movement. The people stay at the front of the worship space for the "Sending Forth Prayer.")

Sending Forth Prayer

God of binding cords and silken ties
    who offers to us hope, friendship, and reconciliation,
send us forth into this world in which brokenness
    and pain are all too prominent.
Help us to be messengers of peace and trust.
Give us courage to live in your love.
May we go in peace and joy, bound together by your
    love. Amen.

(Worship music leaders may play "Bind Us Together" or any other song from the service as the congregation exits.)

(Note: Immediately following the service, consider having a potluck luncheon or other social event where people can gather in informal community to celebrate friendship. If table decorations are needed, use candles with colorful cords around them as centerpieces, carrying the theme of the "Friendship Cords.")

Service 18. "Friendship Cords" Visual Resources and Ideas

DESIGN CONCEPT

In a world in which there are many acquaintances, focus on the sustaining "through thick and thin" power of friendship. Select a simple candlelit table setting with a great number of candles to represent the light of friendship in our lives. The freestanding cross is the centerpiece for this service on which the completed Friendship Cord is placed as part of the worship service.

DESIGN AND DISPLAY SUPPLIES AND RESOURCES

Structure

Use the table length back tabletop riser (66" x 12" x 6").

Fabric

Drape ten yards of white cotton over the back table riser and the table, flowing down in the front of the table. Use tight-weave burlap splashed from the back tabletop riser on the left across the table and down toward the right front of the table. Gather the burlap around the base of the freestanding cross.

Candles

Position ten-inch purple pillar candles at the back corners of the back tabletop riser. Place as many candles as desired on the main level of the table. (We felt it was necessary to have many candles.)

Florals and Plants

On the back tabletop riser, place two rubber tree plants and the large-leafed plant. On the main level of the table, put the spiky plants. Position on each side of the table the Norfolk Island pine trees and the potted palm plants. Set two baskets of artificial ivy on either side of the burlap fabric covering the base of the cross.

Other Items

Place a freestanding cross in front of the table. Drape on the cross the knotted strands of friendship cord. To make the cord, take twelve-inch lengths of cotton clothesline and dye them with watered-down acrylic paints in red, yellow, and blue.

SPECIAL NOTES

The clothesline cords, cut in twelve-inch lengths, will be distributed to the congregation during the worship service. The congregation will then receive instructions regarding the use of the cords.

VISUAL RESOURCES

- Fabric: White cotton and tightly woven burlap, purchased at a local fabric store
- Candles: Purchased at a local craft sore
- Norfolk Island pines: Borrowed from Jerry and Barbara Popp, members of the visual arts team.
- Artificial ivy plants: Borrowed from Nancy Townley
- Lush green plants: Borrowed from Bud's Florist and Greenhouse
- Clothesline cords: Purchased, cut, and dyed by Barbara Popp, a member of the visual arts team
- Rugged cross: Created by Rob Kendall, a member of St. Paul's UMC

WORSHIP RESOURCES

"Bind Us Together," TFWS, no. 2226.

"Hallelujah (Your Love Is Amazing)," DMC songbook, p. 36 and CD, disc A. See also WOW Green songbook, p. 63 and CD, disc 1; or iWOR songbook, CD set, and multiformat trax.

"I Will Be Your Friend" as sung by Michael W. Smith on his *This Is Your Time* CD (Reunion Records). Solo tracks available from Praise Hymn Soundtracks.

"In Unity We Lift Our Song," TFWS, no. 2221.

"Live in Charity," TFWS, no. 2179.

"More than You'll Ever Know" as sung by Watermark. See *WOW 2001, The Year's 30 Top Christian Artists and Songs* CD, silver disc (EMI Christian Music Group). See also Watermark's *All Things New* CD. Visit www.watermarkonline.com for more information.

The Divine Secrets of the Ya-Ya Sisterhood (Warner Brothers and Gaylord Films). Available in DVD and VHS format. Visit www.yayasisterhood.com for more information.

"We Are One in Christ Jesus," TFWS, no. 2229.

"We Are the Body of Christ," TFWS, no. 2227.

"You've Got a Friend" as sung by Carole King on the *Tapestry* CD (CBS Records). See also James Taylor, *Greatest Hits* CD (Warner Bros. Records).

ADDITIONAL RESOURCES

"As the Deer," MGB, no. 89 (especially stanza 2). Stanza 1 only is found in TFWS, no. 2025. See also WOW Orange songbook, p. 7 and CD, cyan disc.

"Draw Me Close," DMC songbook, p. 24 and CD, disc A. See also WOW Green songbook, p. 36 and CD, 2.

"Faithful Friend" as sung by Twila Paris and Steven Curtis Chapman on Twila's *Greatest Hits* CD (Sparrow). Solo cassette tracks also available from Daywind Music Group; order from www.parable.com or your local Christian bookstore.

"How Good and Pleasant," see Tommy Walker's *Never Gonna Stop* songbook and CD, both available from Hosanna! Music. For more information, visit www.integritymusic.com.

"Jesus, Lover of My Soul," WOW Orange songbook, p. 111 and CD, orange. See also iWOR DVD, "D" and multiformat trax.

"Lord, We Come to Ask Your Blessing," TFWS, no. 2230.

"O Look and Wonder," TFWS, no. 2231.

"O the Deep, Deep Love of Jesus," MGB, no. 229. For a great piano version of this hymn, see Craig Curry's *Blue Curry* songbook (Glory Sound), and CD (Radical Middle Music). Instrumental parts also available from Glory Sound.

"Sacred the Body," TFWS, no. 2228.

"What a Friend We Have in Jesus," see Amy Grant's *Legacy, Hymns of Faith* songbook and CD, both published by Word Records). Visit www.wordrecords.com and www.amygrant.com for more information. Solo tracks available from Word Records; visit www.parable.com or your local Christian bookstore.

"Who Is My Mother, Who Is My Brother," TFWS, no. 2225. (This could be used as the closing song.)

Friendship Cords

Musical Invitation: "You've Got a Friend" by Carole King *(Worship Music Leaders or CD)*

Call to Worship
L: We are all children of the one God.
P: We are called to worship together, to share friendship, and to support each other on our faith journeys.
L: Let us celebrate the presence of the One who calls us on the journey.
P: Let us rejoice that we have strong cords of friendship on which to rely.

Songs: "We Are One in Christ Jesus," arranged by Alice Parker
"We Are the Body of Christ" by Scott Wesley Brown and David Hampton

Scripture: Ecclesiastes 4:9-12

Song: "In Unity We Lift Our Song" by Ken Medema *(Stanzas 1 and 2)*

Video Clip from *The Divine Secrets of the Ya-Ya Sisterhood*

Message—Part 1

Song: "I Will Be Your Friend" by Michael W. Smith *(Soloist)*

Message—Part 2

Song: "Hallelujah (Your Love Is Amazing)" by Brenton Brown and Brian Doerksen

Opportunities for Service

Offering: "More Than You'll Ever Know" by Watermark *(Friends montage)*

Prayer Time *(Guided Prayer)*
WL: Lord, remind us that the cords of our being are formed from many single strands:
family, neighborhood, school, friendships.
Each strand by itself possesses certain strengths, but bound together
they become a stronger part of the whole cord.
P: Open our memories to the many strands which make up our individual cords. *(Quiet prayer)*
WL: Lord, we learn to place value on our friendships.
We do not give true friendship lightly.
Trust is crucial in our friendships, and trust is both given and earned.
P: Open our memories to the times in which friendships have been tested. *(Quiet prayer)*
WL: Lord, sometimes friendships can be strained, and we long for healing and restoration, which you alone can provide.
P: Open our hearts and spirits to the need for healing and restoration in our broken friendships. *(Quiet prayer)*
WL: Lord, make room in our hearts for the entrance of others yet unknown to us.
Help us to befriend them and to place a great value on their friendship for your sake.
P: Open our spirits to welcome the strangers who will become beloved friends.
Empower us to be willing to risk friendship in Christ's name. Amen.

Song: "Live in Charity" by Jacques Berthier

Unison Prayer at the End of Prayer Time:
From the very beginning, you desired community for us your people.
You set us apart, O God, to be mirrors of your love.
All through our life journey you give to us people who influence us.
Help us to be models of your love and compassion as we are in community with others. Amen.

Song: "Bind Us Together" by Bob Gillman

Sending Forth Prayer

19. Manna and the Abundant Life

(Holy Communion)

Musical Invitation (*Worship music leaders may play an instrumental version of "Better Is One Day" by Matt Redman, or another appropriate selection.*)

Sung Call to Worship: "Gather Us In," TFWS, no. 2236

Welcome and Opportunities for Service

Song: "Better Is One Day" by Matt Redman (*See WOW Orange.*)

Worship Focus

"What Is It?" (*Skit based on Exodus 16:1-18*)

(*For three male actors: Mesha, Zeke, and Moses*)

Mesha: Moses and Aaron led us away our comfortable houses in Egypt, and for what? For this wasteland! There is nothing here for us. At least we knew what to expect in Egypt.

Zeke: Yeah, we could expect beatings, very low food rations, being separated from our families because the Pharaoh wanted us to build something in someplace or other. Great life, huh?

Mesha: You think this is great? When was your last meal?

Zeke: Okay, so it's been a little while since we've eaten. But we're not dead. Moses said God brought us away from Egypt so we could be free to be God's people. Moses said we should be patient and trust in God. Moses said the time would come when we would enter the promised land—

Mesha: (*Sarcastically*) Moses said, Moses said! We were stupid to follow that phony! What's he going to give us for dinner?

Zeke: Just wait. Something will happen.

Mesha: Yeah, like funerals. At least the circling vultures will feast well tonight!

Zeke: Looks like circling quails to me.

Mesha: Huh?

Zeke: Look over there. (*Zeke points and Mesha looks.*) And what's that white stuff on the grass?

Mesha: It shouldn't take a Pharaoh to figure that out!

Zeke: (*Undeterred*) Let's get a closer look. (*Zeke and Mesha move toward Moses.*)

Moses: You may eat this manna—it is a gift from God. Don't hoard it; just take what you need for the day. There will be more tomorrow.

Zeke: Sounds good to me. (*Pantomimes picking up the manna and eating.*) This stuff doesn't taste too bad either. (*Hands some to Mesha who eats it and frowns.*)

Mesha: Who does he think he's kidding? There won't be enough for tomorrow! I'm going to take all I can carry right now and come back for more. Let those fools gather the manna tomorrow, if there's any to gather!

Zeke: (*Sighs*) Some people don't know a good thing, even when it's bread from heaven!

Message Movers

In the midst of the wilderness, God offered the hungry Israelites manna, a mysterious substance that would feed and sustain the people. But there were restrictions: take only what you need for the day; do not take more than you need—you will have enough.

But when the people took more than they needed, the manna rotted! (It's always best to pay attention to what God says!)

We are taught that it is best to "save for a rainy day." If we can just put enough of whatever it is we are gathering aside, we will be safe. So, like the ancient Israelites who were hungry and didn't know where the next meal was coming from, we probably would have done the same thing. We would gather as much as we could. We might even wonder if God was kidding and testing us to see if we were smart enough to "hedge our bet."

We are so mistrustful of God's abundant care for us that we want assurances. Couldn't God give us a sign, a document, a guarantee? God did give the assurance—daily manna in the wilderness—as promised. What are we looking for?

The motto of our faith is the same as the motto for the state of Missouri: "Show Me." We have to have proof.

The proof is in our trust. Abundant life is for those who are willing to trust in God's providence. It is not in our ability to collect or horde the blessings.

Song: "Deep in the Shadows of the Past," TFWS, no. 2246

Segue into Sharing Holy Communion
Just as the Hebrew people wandered in the
    wilderness,
        learning to trust God and rely on God's provi-
        sion for them,
Jesus' disciples hungered and thirsted
        for that which would sustain them.
One evening, as they were gathered in a borrowed
        upper room,
Jesus gave his disciples a meal
        that would nourish their souls and heal their
        broken spirits.

Sharing Holy Communion

(The pastor uncovers the bread and the wine. Lifting up the bread, the pastor says:)

On the night that Jesus was betrayed, he took bread and lifted it toward heaven saying: "Blessed are you, O Lord God of the universe, who has offered to us the grain of the field from which this bread is made." Then he blessed the bread and broke it, giving it to his disciples, saying: "Take, eat. This is my body, which is broken for you. Do this in remembrance of me."

(The pastor places the bread back on the plate. Lifting up the cup, the pastor says:)

Likewise, after supper Jesus took the cup, lifted it toward heaven and said:
"Blessed are you, O Lord God of the universe, who has given to us the fruit of the vine from which this wine is made." Then he blessed the cup and gave it to his disciples, saying: "Drink from this, all of you, for this is my blood of the new covenant, which is poured out for you and for many for the forgiveness of sins. Do this in remembrance of me."

In remembrance of Christ's incredible love for us, we celebrate this holy meal. The table of the Lord is open to everyone. Come out of your wilderness. Be healed, and receive with abundant joy and confidence the manna from heaven.

(The people receive the elements in the manner common to your congregation.)

Songs: "All Who Hunger," TFWS, no. 2126
        "Life-giving Bread," TFWS, no. 2261

Segue into Offering
As Christ has offered his life for us,
        let us offer our gifts in Christ's name,
so that his healing love may be known
        through the ministries of this church.

Offering: "Bread from Heaven" by J. Paul Williams
        and Ruth Elaine Schram

(Consider using this piece, written in a Caribbean style, with a small SATB vocal ensemble, piano, and percussion. Add bass guitar and steel drums using a MIDI keyboard patch, if possible.)

Prayer Time

(The worship leader leads the following prayer and invites the congregation to offer joys and concerns in selected spots.)

O Bread of Life, who feeds our hungry souls,
        we praise you for nourishing us with your great
        and boundless love.
We lift to you the celebrations with which you have
        graced our lives,
        and we offer thanks for the blessings of joy and
        love.

(Invite the congregation to share joys here.)

O Living Bread, who makes us whole,
        we lift to you the concerns that are on our hearts
        today.
We ask for your healing power, for hope, and for
        comfort.

(Invite the congregation to share concerns here.)

Take all these things, O Lord,
        for we place our trust and gratitude in you.
        Amen.

Segue into Closing Song
As Christ has given himself for us,
        let us give our lives for him.
"Let us be bread, blessed by the Lord,
        Let us be wine, love freely poured."

Closing Song: "Let Us Be Bread," TFWS, no. 2260

Sending Forth *(From "Let Us Be Bread")*

(The pastor or worship leader may read stanzas 3 and 4 of "Let Us Be Bread" as a Sending Forth. See the Singer's Edition of TFWS.)

(The worship music leaders may play "Let Us Be Bread" as the congregation exits.)

Service 19. "Manna and the Abundant Life" Visual Resources and Ideas

DESIGN CONCEPT

We are so much like the wandering Israelites in Exodus. We are led to certain destinations, and then we complain because we don't have everything we want. We wonder if God will take care of us. The worship visual design for this service is reminiscent of the Exodus event and the provisions that God makes for us.

DESIGN AND DISPLAY SUPPLIES AND RESOURCES

Structure

Set up the back tabletop riser. Create additional risers upon which to display the bush on which "manna" was found, as well as the brass cross.

Fabric

Drape the back tabletop riser and the whole table with approximately ten yards of white cotton fabric. Overlay landscaper's burlap, creating a rustic and earthy look.

Candles

Four candles are needed. On the top riser, use two 6-inch white pillar candles, placed slightly behind the stack of breads. Put a 4-inch white pillar candle in the center of the main table level. To the extreme right, place the 6-inch burgundy candle.

Florals and Plants

The only living plants in this display are the two spiky plants on the upper back table top riser, to the extreme right. Create a bush out of branches that are placed in a black plastic pot filled with floral foam; use rocks to anchor it.

Other Items

On the back tabletop riser, set a basket on its side and place some bread spilling out of it, toward the left of the setting. Place additional loaves of bread in the center of the table. Position the "manna bush" on a riser. Devise manna by using polyester fiberfill (quilt stuffing) in little clusters, and snag it on the branches. Open a large Bible and rest it against the riser for the manna bush. On the right side of the main level of the table, place the brass cross on the other riser. In front of it, add an earthenware chalice (cup) and paten (plate). Place the communion bread on the plate. Clusters of artificial grapes surrounded the cross and the chalice. At the base of the table, put three large rocks to anchor the design.

SPECIAL NOTES

This is a wonderfully expressive table. Unfortunately in this design, the worship leader cannot conduct the communion liturgy from behind the table, due to the placement of the riser and the other artifacts. The communion elements are on the table, but they are not covered. If this is problematic for the worship leader or pastor, a small linen cloth should suffice without compromising the integrity of the setting. Following the communion, the unused breads may be distributed to members of the congregation.

VISUAL RESOURCES

- Fabric: White cotton, purchased at local fabric store; landscaper's burlap, purchased at a landscaping center
- Candles: Purchased at a local craft store
- Breads: Purchased at a local supermarket
- Brass cross, chalice and paten: Belong to St. Paul's UMC
- Spiky plants: Borrowed from Bud's Florist and Greenhouse
- Artificial grapes and bread basket: Borrowed from Nancy Townley
- Rocks: Borrowed from Jerry Popp, a member of the visual arts team

WORSHIP RESOURCES

"All Who Hunger," TFWS, no. 2126.

"Better Is One Day," WOW Orange songbook, p. 13 and CD, orange disc.

"Bread from Heaven" by J. Paul Williams and Ruth Elaine Schram (Glory Sound, a division of Shawnee Press, Inc.), SATB with parts for Latin percussion.

"Deep in the Shadows of the Past," TFWS, no. 2246.

"Gather Us In," TFWS, no. 2236.

"Let Us Be Bread," TFWS, no. 2260.

"Life-giving Bread," TFWS, no. 2261.

ADDITIONAL RESOURCES

"As We Gather at Your Table," TFWS, no. 2268.

"Celebration Song," CC, no. 85.

"Change My Heart, O God," TFWS, no. 2152. See also DMC songbook, p. 13 and CD, disc B; MGB, no. 16; or WOW Blue songbook, p. 20 and CD, yellow disc.

"Come and Taste," CC, no. 82.

"Come, Let Us Eat," UMH, no. 625.

"Come Out the Wilderness," UMH, no. 416. See also Songs of Zion (Abingdon Press), no. 136.

"Come to the Table," TFWS, no. 2264.

"God Is Good All the Time," WOW Orange songbook, p. 35 and CD, cyan disc.

"Hungry," DMC songbook, p. 43 and CD, disc A. See also WOW Orange songbook, p. 63 and CD, orange disc; or iWOR multiformat trax.

"I Don't Feel No Ways Tired," by Curtis Burrell, *Songs of Zion* (Abingdon Press), no. 175.

"Lead On, O Cloud of Presence," TFWS, no. 2234.

"Song of the Body of Christ," by David Haas, *You Are Mine* collection, Vol. 2 (GIA Publications, Inc.), available in CD and cassette format.

"Taste and See," TFWS, no. 2267.

"You Who Are Thirsty," TFWS, no. 2132.

Manna and the Abundant Life

Musical Invitation *(Worship Music Leaders)*

Sung Call to Worship: "Gather Us In" by Marty Haugen

Welcome and Opportunities for Service

Song: "Better Is One Day" by Matt Redman

Worship Focus

"What Is It?" *(Skit based on Exodus 16:1-18)*

Message

Song: "Deep in the Shadows of the Past" by Brian Wren

Sharing Holy Communion

  Songs: "All Who Hunger" by Sylvia G. Dunstan and William Moore
    "Life-giving Bread" by Ricky Manalo

  Offering: "Bread from Heaven" by J. Paul Williams and Ruth Elaine Schram
    (Musical ensemble)

Prayer Time

Closing Song: "Let Us Be Bread" by Thomas Porter

Sending Forth

20. The Keeper of the Bread

(Communion/World Communion Sunday)

Musical Invitation (*Worship music leaders may play an instrumental version of "Holy" or another appropriate selection, perhaps something from another culture. If you would like to play a CD, consider Craig Curry's jazz arrangement of "All Hail the Power of Jesus' Name." See Worship Resources for more information.*)

Welcome and Greeting One Another

Songs: "All Hail the Power of Jesus' Name," UMH, no. 154
(*See also MGB, no. 2; or iWOR DVD. Use the iWOR version, if possible.*)
"Holy," TFWS, no. 2019

Worship Focus (*Worship Leader*)

Central to so many of the world's people is table fellowship, although there may be no table but rather a gathering place to share a common meal. In today's worship, we offer three tables. The central table is the Lord's Table, with its emphasis on communion celebration. The breads are from many nations, representing the body of Christ. Several varieties of grapes remind us of the blood of Christ.

In front of the communion table and to the left, we will set an elegant table as a reminder of all those who have received abundantly in this life. This table is set with the finest china. It is a table truly fit for a royal guest. Conversely, on the table to the right of the communion table, the setting will be simple and rustic—representing those who have little, only the basic needs for survival.

All of the people represented by these two tables are invited to the central table where Christ does not differentiate between wealth and poverty. Our communion stewards represent both the fortunate and the impoverished people. They come to the table bringing the best that they have, which will be blessed by the Lord. These gifts will be equally shared. No one is left out. We are invited to come to the table of the Lord where the Keeper of the Bread offers a feast to satisfy all people.

Song: "Life-giving Bread," TFWS, no. 2261 (stanzas 1 and 2)
(*Sing two refrains at the beginning, stanza 1, refrain, stanza 2, and two refrains.*)

(*Select four persons to serve as communion stewards. During the singing of "Life-giving Bread," each pair of stewards brings in one plate with the communion bread and one chalice with the grape juice. They place the items on the central table—Table 1. The plate and chalice on the congregation's left are fancy, and the plate and chalice on the congregation's right are plain, preferably earthenware. When the items are in place, the stewards should cover them with a linen cloth. Then the stewards return to their seats in the congregation.*)

Message Movers—Part 1

Bread, sometimes called the "staff of life," is a staple in many cultures. On our communion table today are breads from all over the world. Each culture has its own specialty bread, such as: Portuguese sweet bread, Irish soda bread, pita bread, braided challah, sourdough bread, Italian bread, and French baguettes. Dinner tables are set with bread, some for the common meal, others reserved for special meals and celebration occasions.

The word *Lord* is often used interchangeably with "Jesus." The origins of the word come from the Old English words *hlaf*, meaning bread or loaf, and *weard*, meaning keeper. In the Middle Ages, the Lord was the keeper of the loaf; the one who protected and provided the essentials for survival and health.

Jesus, our Lord, is the keeper and giver of the bread, which gives life and sustenance. He has offered himself—the Bread of Life—to us for our salvation, for forgiveness, for restoration. We don't take that offering lightly or for granted.

Each time we come to the table, we come to a celebration of this gift of life. We are offered a place at the table free of charge. In the sacrament of Holy Communion, we are invited to the one table—everyone; no one is excluded from the bread of life. There is always room at Christ's table.

What would we do if Christ came to our own tables in our homes? Consider the wonderful story about a boy and his family who regularly spent Easter holidays with the boy's grandmother. He noted that the children's table was always separate from the adults. One Easter, he noticed a special change—there was no children's table. The adult table had been enlarged to include the children. When the family was seated for dinner, the boy saw that one chair and place setting were empty, and he asked his grandmother about it. She said a Jewish friend told her that Jewish families typically set an extra place at the table in case Elijah returned. It is called happy hospitality. So she decided that if Jesus returned and entered her house, she would want Jesus to know that all the members of the family were seated together and that there was always a place for Jesus. The boy and his family carried that memory and tradition with them from that moment onward.

If Christ came to dinner at our homes, how would we prepare our table for him?

Setting the Table for a Special Guest (Table 2)
(For Worship Leader [WL] and seven presenters [PR])

(Facing the central table from the congregation, Table 2 is set on the main floor to the left. As each item is brought forward, the presenter reads the corresponding line and places the item on the table. The presenters return to their place in the congregation.)

WL: How shall we set the table for a special guest?

PR 1: I bring to this table a cloth, given to me by my mother. It was her best tablecloth and was used only on special occasions.

PR 2: I bring to this table our best dinner plates. We always knew the event was important when the special china was brought out.

PR 3: I bring to this table our best crystal goblets. The light they reflect is beautiful and they ring true, as good crystal glass does. These are only for momentous occasions.

PR 4: I bring to this table our silver service. Mother used this only on the most significant of occasions. It was carefully polished and made ready for our guests.

PR 5: I bring to this table our lovely cloth napkins, carefully ironed and placed in special napkin rings on each plate, awaiting use by our dear friends.

PR 6: I bring to this table a vase of flowers, fragrant and delicate, gracing our table.

PR 7: I bring to this table two candles in crystal holders, reminders of elegance and light.

Song: "Life-giving Bread," TFWS, no. 2261 (stanzas 3 and 4)
(Sing two refrains at the beginning, stanza 3, refrain, stanza. 4, and two refrains.)

Message Movers—Part 2

The table we have just set is impressive. We have gone to a great deal of trouble to impress Jesus. Only the best cloth, china, and crystal have been used. To sit at this table is to be treated to the best a family can offer.

Each culture of the world would find a special way to set the table for Christ. Great care would be taken to make sure everything is "just right." And although elegant hospitality is a great gift to offer guests, Christ is looking for something else, the hospitality of the heart.

The Lord's table set before us is a table of true elegance and simplicity. The Lord who said "Take, eat; this bread is my body broken for you," brings us back to the basics. He who is the source of life has offered life to us for our salvation, for forgiveness, for restoration. The fancy china, the glittering crystal, the glowing silver, and the warmth of the candles pale in comparison to the power of the symbols of the bread.

When we least expect it, the bread is offered for us. We taste its flavor; as we roll it in our mouths, we experience its texture; we inhale its aroma. It is real.

Each day we are reminded that the keeper of the bread continually feeds us. We are fed out of God's great love and generosity. The bread enters our lives and builds us up in service to the one who offered all. Strengthened by this bread, we are poured out in service to the hungering and thirsting world—to offer the bread of life to others.

Setting the Table of Mercy and Thanksgiving (Table 3)
(For Worship Leader [WL] and four presenters [PR])

(Facing the central table from the congregation, Table 3 is set on the main floor to the right. As each item is brought forward, the presenter reads the corresponding line and places the item on the table. The presenters return to their place in the congregation.)

WL: How shall we set the table of mercy and thanksgiving for our Lord?

PR 1: I bring to this table a simple cloth, representing the simple gift of love.

PR 2: I bring to this table an earthenware plate on which a loaf of bread has been placed, representing the body of Christ, born from this earth.

PR 3: I bring to this table an earthenware cup in which the juice of the grape has been poured, representing the blood of Christ poured out for us.

PR 4: I bring to this table a candle in a wooden holder, representing the light of the world who gives his life for us.

(The keyboardist begins playing "Come to the Table" as soon as the last line above is spoken. When the presenters have returned to their seats, the Worship Leader begins the segue, with the keyboardist still playing. As soon as the segue is over, the congregation sings "Come to the Table" two times.)

Segue to Communion: "Come and Get It" *(Worship Leader)*

"Come and Get It!" Does that call sound familiar to
> you?
It is often used to call children to the table.
They come tumbling in, looking forward to the
> meal.
The Keeper of the Bread,
> the Christ who offers his finest wheat, his whole
> life for you,
> invites you to come to the table.
For this bread is none other than the body of Christ;
> this cup is none other than the blood of Christ.
Dear friends, come and get it!
The holy meal is ready for you.

Song: "Come to the Table," TFWS, no. 2264 *(Sing two times.)*

Sharing the Table of Holy Communion (Table 1)
(During the singing of "Come to the Table," the Pastor enters and stands behind the central table [Table 1]. Two sets of communion stewards enter and stand on each side of the pastor.)

Presenting the Elements
Pastor: Welcome to the Lord's table, set for you. In this moment, we remember a time long ago when Jesus, at dinner with his disciples, took bread, and offered a prayer of thanksgiving for it.

(At this point, the keyboardist begins playing at measure 5 of "Broken for Me" while the Pastor readies the bread.)

(Four measures later, the Pastor or soloist sings stanza 3 of "Broken for Me" as the Pastor takes the bread, lifts it up, blesses it, and breaks it, showing it to the gathered people. Then he or she replaces it on the plate. The keyboardist plays the refrain as the Pastor readies the cup. The next line is read at measure 5 of the refrain.)

Pastor: Likewise after the meal, Jesus took the cup and offered it to his disciples.

(The Pastor or soloist sings stanza 4 of "Broken for Me" as the Pastor takes the cup, lifts it up, blesses it, and shows it to the gathered people. Then he or she places it on the table. At the end of the verse, the congregation joins in the sung response below.)

Sung Response: "Broken for Me," TFWS, no. 2263
(Refrain, stanza 1, refrain, stanza 2, refrain, and CODA)

(During the singing of the response, the two pairs of communion stewards move to the main floor. The stewards on the congregation's left will stand beside the elegant table [Table 2]. The stewards on the congregation's right will stand beside the plain table [Table 3].)

Sharing the Elements
(The sharing of the elements should be offered by intinction. The bread steward breaks the bread and asks the first name of the congregant. The steward repeats the name as he or she hands the bread to the congregant saying, "NAME, this is the body of Christ broken for you." The congregant dips the bread in the chalice, as the chalice steward says, "The blood of Christ poured out for you." The congregant eats the bread and then returns to his or her seat. This pattern continues until all have been served. Then the communion stewards serve each other. They return to the central table. One pair of stewards serves the bread to the Pastor; one pair offers the cup. When the Pastor has received communion, the elements are placed on the table but not covered. The stewards return to their seats.)

Songs: "Come, Let Us Eat," UMH no. 625
(Feature a strong "Leader" and African percussion instruments. If you don't have African instruments, have someone clap or stomp a rhythm or play a hand drum.)
> "Come, Share the Lord," TFWS, no. 2269
> *(Soloist)*
> "Sing Alleluia to the Lord," TFWS, no. 2258

Prayer following Communion
(The Pastor should prepare this prayer, perhaps using some of the language from "One Bread, One Body.")

Song: "One Bread, One Body," UMH, no. 620 or CC, no. 84)

Prayer Time
(Prayers of the People—intercessory prayers. To incorporate music, consider using "Prayers of the People" or "The Fragrance of Christ." If using "The Fragrance of Christ," sing it at the beginning of the prayer time, with the congregation singing each refrain and a soloist offering the verses. The keyboardist would continue to play the verses softly during the intercessions, and the congregation would respond with the refrain. See Worship Resources for information on these songs.)

Segue into Opportunities for Service:
How can we feed the community with the bread of
> life,
> of friendship, of reconciliation?
There are many ways to offer nurture and
> sustenance

through the ministries and missions of this congregation.
There is a place for you to serve, and in serving, to be fed.
Open your hearts to these opportunities.

Opportunities for Service

Segue into Offering:

Now that we have been fed, let us bring our gifts before the Lord.

Offering/Closing Song: "Let Us Offer to the Father," TFWS, no. 2262

(If possible, accompany the song primarily with acoustic guitar and Latin percussion instruments. Worship music leaders may sing the song in Spanish, using as many verses as necessary until the offering is collected. If there are no Spanish-speaking persons in the congregation, consider asking a high school student who is taking Spanish to offer the spoken words with the music playing underneath. When the offering is collected, play one refrain during which time the Worship Leader invites the congregation to stand and sing the entire song in English.)

Sending Forth

We have been fed and nourished by the Lord,
the Keeper and Giver of the Bread of Life.
Let us go forth into the world
with joy to serve all God's people.
Go in peace and joy. Amen.

(Worship music leaders may play "Let Us Offer to the Father" as the congregation exits.)

Service 20. "The Keeper of the Bread" Visual Resources and Ideas

DESIGN CONCEPT

This design started small and then took on a life of its own. It started with a simple central table (Table 1) on which many breads from different parts of the world would be placed. We decided to incorporate the world and cross panel that we used in a design for Advent. The traditional altar candles were placed on either side of the panel. As we discussed the service, we realized that all people are called to Christ's table, and so we chose to symbolize the wealth and poverty of the world by creating two tables to be placed in front of the central table. Table 2, on the left, is the elegant table, focusing on those who are blessed with abundance. Table 3, on the right, is the rustic and simple table, representing those who struggle to survive.

DESIGN AND DISPLAY SUPPLIES AND RESOURCES

Structure

Use the back tabletop riser for the altar candles. Behind the back riser, mount the panel on an artists' easel supported by two milk cartons. The tables in the foreground (Table 2 and 3) are actually piano benches. These tables are for display only and will not be used, so they can be lower than the central table.

Fabric

Cover the back tabletop riser and the whole central table with ten yards of white cotton fabric. "Swag" the material over the front of the table. On Table 2, the elegant table, use mauve colored fabric and a lace tablecloth. On Table 3, place the tea-dyed cloth.

Candles

Position traditional altar candles on the top of the back table riser. On Table 2, add a lovely pink floral candle. On Table 3, set a small, off-white pillar candle.

Florals and Plants

The back tabletop riser has two small Boston ferns to soften the edges of the panel and give a break between the panel and the large candlesticks. On either side of the central table, place the potted palm plants. In front of the left front of Table 2, set a basket of pink artificial roses. In front of the right front of Table 3, put a basket of wheat sheaves.

Other Items

The traditional brass chalice rests on a riser in the center of the central table. A panel depicting the earth and the cross of Christ (acrylic painting on room darkening fabric) is behind the top riser. Breads from many nations grace the center table, with a cluster of artificial grapes spilling over the center edge of the table. Put two sheaves of wheat at each end of the central table. The elegant table (Table 2) is set with fine china, silverware, crystal goblet, and linen napkin. Table 3 is set with an earthenware plate, a mug, a paper napkin, a cracked milk jug, and mismatched silverware.

SPECIAL NOTES

This set takes awhile to create. As in Service 19, the pastor does not consecrate the communion elements directly behind the table, but rather to the side. See the directions in the worship service.

VISUAL RESOURCES

• Fabric: White, mauve, and tea-dyed cotton, purchased at a local fabric store

- Lace tablecloth and linen napkin: Borrowed from Barbara Popp, a member of the visual arts team
- Altar candles: Belong to St. Paul's UMC
- Pink floral candle and off-white pillar candle: Borrowed from Barbara Popp
- Cross and earth panel: Created by Nancy Townley and painted by Lesley Leonard, a member of the visual arts team
- Breads: Purchased at a local supermarket
- Sheaves of wheat, wheat basket, crystal goblet and grapes: Borrowed from Nancy Townley
- Ferns and potted palms: Borrowed from Bud's Florist and Greenhouse
- Elegant china dishes, silverware, cup and saucer: Belong to St. Paul's UMC
- Brass chalice: Belongs to St. Paul's UMC
- Earthenware dish and mug, milk pitcher, and pink rose basket: Borrowed from Barbara Popp
- Two additional chalices (cups) with grape juice and two additional patens (plates) with bread. These items will be brought forward by the two sets of communion stewards.

WORSHIP RESOURCES

"All Hail the Power of Jesus' Name," UMH, no. 154. See also MGB, no. 2; or iWOR DVD, "A," songbook, and multiformat trax. For a jazz instrumental version, see Craig Curry's *Blue Curry* CD (Radical Middle Music).

"Broken for Me," TFWS, no. 2263.

"Come, Let Us Eat," UMH, no. 625.

"Come to the Table," TFWS, no. 2264.

"Come, Share the Lord" by Bryan Jeffery Leech, TFWS, no. 2269. An arrangement by Roland Tabell, with a nice piano accompaniment, is found in *The Communion Soloist* (Fred Bock Music Company).

"Holy," TFWS, no. 2019.

"Let Us Offer to the Father," TFWS, no. 2262.

"Life-Giving Bread," TFWS, no. 2261.

"One Bread, One Body," see: UMH, no. 620 or CC, no. 84.

"Prayers of the People," TFWS, no. 2201.

"Sing Alleluia to the Lord," TFWS, no. 2258.

"The Fragrance of Christ," see: TFWS, no. 2205 or CC, no. 34.

"You Who Are Thirsty," TFWS, no. 2132.

ADDITIONAL RESOURCES

"All You Who Are Thirsty," CC, no. 86.

"As We Gather at Your Table," TFWS, no. 2268.

"Bread for the World" by Bernadette Farrell (Oregon Catholic Press Publications), song with parts for keyboard, guitar, and clarinet. See also the *God Beyond All Names* collection, available in CD or cassette format.

"Celebration Song," CC, no. 85.

"Come and Taste," CC, no. 82.

"Come Just as You Are," MGB, no. 179. See also WOW Green songbook, p. 26 and CD, disc 2.

"I Will Remember You," CC, no. 81.

"Light of the World," TFWS, no. 2204.

"Think about His Love," WOW Green songbook, p. 138 and CD, disc 2.

"The Invitation," by Steven Curtis Chapman, *Speechless* (Hal Leonard Corporation), p. 65. CD available from Sparrow Records. For more information, visit www.scchapman.com.

"Time Now to Gather," TFWS, no. 2265.

"We Come to Your Feast," by Michael Joncas (GIA Publications, Inc.), arrangement for two or three voices, cantor, congregation, guitar, keyboard, and optional flute or oboe; instrumental parts also available. See also the collection, *We Come to Your Feast* (GIA Publications, Inc.); available in CD or cassette format. (You can hear this song on the GIA website.)

"We Gather in Worship," by Sylvia G. Dunstan and Bob Moore (GIA Publications, Inc.), a gospel style arrangement for SATB voices, congregation, descant, guitar, and keyboard. Also available on Bob Moore's *When the Lord in Glory Comes,* in CD or cassette format.

"You Satisfy the Hungry Heart," UMH, no. 629.

The Keeper of the Bread

Musical Invitation *(Worship Music Leaders)*

Welcome and Greeting One Another

Songs: "All Hail the Power of Jesus' Name" by Edward Perronet and Oliver Holden
"Holy" by Guillermo Cuéllar

Worship Focus

Song: "Life-giving Bread," by Ricky Manalo *(Stanzas 1 and 2)*

Message—Part 1

Setting the Table for a Special Guest

Song: "Life-giving Bread" *(Stanzas 3 and 4)*

Message—Part 2

Setting the Table of Mercy and Thanksgiving

Song: "Come to the Table" by Claire Cloninger and Martin J. Nystrom *(Sing twice.)*

Sharing the Table of Holy Communion

Presenting the Elements

Sung Response: "Broken for Me" by Janet Lunt *(Refrain, Stanza 1, Refrain, Stanza 2, Refrain, and CODA)*

Sharing the Elements

Songs: "Come, Let Us Eat" by Billema Kwillia
"Come, Share the Lord" by Bryan Jeffery Leech *(Soloist)*
"Sing Alleluia to the Lord" by Linda Stassen

Prayer

Song: "One Bread, One Body" by John B. Foley

Prayer Time

Opportunities for Service

Offering/Closing Song: "Let Us Offer to the Father" *(From the* Misa Popular Nicaragüense*)*

Sending Forth

Music Resources

Out of the plethora of worship materials available, we chose several and used them rather extensively throughout *Praise Now! 2*. We understand that budget restraints often prohibit the purchase of multiple, expensive resources. Consequently, we have chosen resources that give great "bang for the buck." Many of the songs suggested in this guide are contained in several of the resources listed below, so you won't need to purchase all the resources. Simply choose the ones that best suit your needs.

If you find only one or two songs in a collection that you wish to use, check CCLI's lead sheet service and www.praisecharts.com for lead sheets (melody line and guitar chords) of individual songs, or contact your local Christian music store for information regarding the availability of sheet music. If you are unable to locate music for the song(s) in question, write the copyright holders (often the publisher)

and ask for permission to reprint. Most publishers have a website that can be found by simply typing the publisher's name into your search engine. State clearly when and how you plan to use the song(s) and how many copies you need to make. Sometimes songs in a collection are available for purchase separately. The copyright holder will let you know if this is the case with the song(s) you've selected, or they will either grant or deny you permission to reprint. Most copyright holders will grant permission for a small fee.

Complete resource information is listed here, including the abbreviations used throughout this guide. These resources as well as other resources listed throughout this publication are available through your local music store, Christian bookstore, or through a variety of Internet based suppliers.

BOW   Langford, Andy, ed. *The United Methodist Book of Worship*. Nashville: The United Methodist Publishing House, 1992. Visit www.cokesbury.com or call 1-800-672-1789 for more information.

CC   Townley, Cathy and Mike Graham. *Come Celebrate! Music for Contemporary Worship*, Songbook 1. Nashville: Abingdon Press, 1995. The CD includes fifteen of the songs in the songbook. Visit www.cokesbury.com or call 1-800-672-1789 for more information.

CCJ   Townley, Cathy. *Come Celebrate! Jesus! Music for Contemporary Worship*. Nashville: Abingdon Press, 1997. Visit www.cokesbury.com or call 1-800-672-1789 for more information.

DMC   *Draw Me Close: 25 Top Vineyard Worship Songs*. Vineyard Music. Songbook includes piano, vocals, and guitar chords; double CD set sold separately. For more information, visit www.vineyardonline.com.

iWOR   *iWorship* resources are published by Integrity. CDs feature popular worship songs; an enhanced songbook containing all the songs on the CDs; multiformat trax of songs (presented in five versions and three keys); and DVDs featuring selected worship songs complete with graphics and lyrics. For more information, visit www.iworshipnow.com or call 1-866-WORSHIP.

MGB   *Maranatha! Music Praise Hymns and Choruses*, 4th Edition ("*Green Book*"). This resource comes in many formats, including: classic songbook, reference CD, singalong book, MIDI files, split-track rehearsal CDs, and a variety of arrangements for worship band and worship teams. To find out which version is best for you, contact Maranatha! Music at 1-800-245-SONG or visit www.maranathamusic.com.

OGR   *Our God Reigns, The Praise and Worship Collection* Songbook. Milwaukee: Hal Leonard Corporation. For more information, visit www.halleonard.com.

TFWS   Hickman, Hoyt L., ed. *The Faith We Sing*. Nashville: Abingdon Press, 2000. Available in various print and electronic editions. For more information, visit www.thefaithwesing.com, www.cokesbury.com, or call Cokesbury at 1-800-672-1789.

UMH   Young, Carlton R., ed. *The United Methodist Hymnal*. Nashville: The United Methodist Publishing House, 1989. Visit www.cokesbury.com or call 1-800-672-1789 for more information.

WA   Smith, Michael W., *Worship Again* Songbook. Nashville: Brentwood-Benson Music Publishing. CD available from Reunion Records. For more information, visit www.michaelwsmith.com and www.reunionrecords.com.

WOW   *Worship Songbook* (Blue). Mobile, Ala.: Integrity Incorporated, 1999. CD also available. For more information, visit www.integritymusic.com or www.wowworship.com.

WOW   *WOW Christmas Songbook, 30 Top Christian Artists and Holiday Songs* (Christmas). Nashville: Word Music, 2002. CD also available. For more information, visit www.wowchristmas.com.

WOW   *WOW Worship Songbook* (Green). Mobile, Ala.: Integrity Incorporated, 2001. CD also available. For more information, visit www.integritymusic.com or www.wowworship.com.

WOW   *WOW Worship Songbook* (Orange). Mobile, Ala.: Integrity Incorporated, 2000. CD also available. For more information, visit www.integritymusic.com or www.wowworship.com.

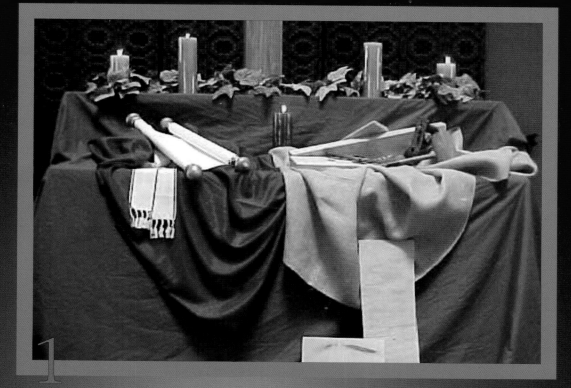

1

2

3

12

13

14

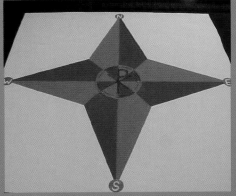

15